THE RICH RECRUITER

◆

How to win in recruitment

Andrew Leong

CONTENTS

INTRODUCTION

When I began as a recruitment consultant I searched for books, people, videos, articles: anything and everything that would make me a successful recruiter, fast. I spent a considerable amount of time looking for that "golden" method, or a method that would bring me instant success and fortune. Unfortunately, I never found such a book, and the majority of titles I read were sales orientated. Although these books were highly beneficial, recruitment is unlike selling a product. Recruitment is far more complex with many psychological obstacles. What I needed was a book specifically dealing with recruitment; one that was not watered down in any way, and that remained completely true to the industry.

After rigorous training, mentoring and on the job experience, in addition to having spent a considerable amount of time carefully observing successful recruiters, I've accumulated the secrets: all the tips and tricks of the top recruiters. I've recorded these tools, techniques and best practices for you in this book. When you combine these with working smart, you have an effective framework used by the most successful recruitment consultants at your fingertips.

In this book, I've broken up the recruitment process into manageable, bite-sized categories; structuring it in a way that allows you to easily find what you need for most of the problems you will face in recruitment.

I'll tell you what to say to increase your reputation as a recruiter, close meetings and win clients. I'll tell you how to find candidates and decision makers, how to send e-shots that'll pull in jobs and how to make yourself indispensable to your company.

One of my main motivations for writing this book is that selling is a skill and like any skill it can be learnt and improved through practice. It is a common misconception that selling is a natural talent. While there are naturally talented people in all aspects of life, including sales, the saying goes:

"Hard work beats talent when talent doesn't work hard"

I'm not a natural sales person, but through hard work, education and experience I was able to develop the necessary skills and confidence to close deals.

If you're new to recruitment, this book is a guide to help you up a steep learning curve. The fact that you've bought this book already demonstrates you have some of the qualities of a successful recruitment consultant.

If you're an experienced recruitment consultant, this book will provide you with new ideas to implement into your existing recruitment process, and remind you of the basics that can sometimes be forgotten.

You'll notice that there is some repetition within the book. I've separated the tools and techniques of recruitment for easy reference, but in some cases there's a natural crossover as the book progresses. At the same time I've made a conscious effort to repeat certain topics for emphasis: it's all too easy to read an important topic once, only to forget about it several pages later.

This book is divided into three parts.

Part One – An introduction to recruitment. If you're

an experienced recruitment consultant you can skip the second two sections of this part of the book.

Part Two – Sales. This part will equip you with the necessary tools and techniques for selling within the recruitment industry.

Part Three – A methodology for recruitment. You can have all the tools you need to build a house, but it doesn't mean you'll be **able** to build a house. What you need is a guide on how to use those tools. The third part of the book shows you just that. Whether you're new to recruitment or already experienced, if you're not getting the sales you expect it's possible that your approach is misaligned. This part of the book will ensure you're on the right track to becoming a rich recruiter.

PART 1

ABOUT

RECRUITMENT

A SUCCESSFUL
RECRUITMENT CONSULTANT

What makes a successful recruitment consultant? Can you replicate their success? I've found that the best recruitment consultants are successful for several reasons:

People skills – They're good with people. They can read people's emotions over the telephone, in person and even through written text. They show empathy and concern when it's necessary, but they also share people's happiness and excitement.

Opportunities – Good recruitment consultants can spot opportunities for doing business.

Organisation – You've got candidates to manage, clients to call back, candidates to interview, clients to visit, CV's to write, job adverts to put out, targets to hit and mass amounts of information to remember. The best recruitment consultants are highly organised to make everything flow, most of the time.

Tenacity – Recruitment is a rough, tough and competitive industry. Competing agencies are calling **your** candidates and **your** clients. Gatekeepers are trying to keep you out. Candidates can drop out of placements or get rejected by your clients. All recruitment consultants go through these problems, but the successful ones move quickly forward past any setbacks.

Teamwork – Good recruitment consultants don't work in isolation, they ask for help from colleagues to utilise their time better. They'll also help their teammates, creating a strong collaborative working environment.

Hard work – Successful recruitment consultants are hard workers. They'll work late nights or early mornings to get the job finished. They're also smart workers. They'll work hard on the right things at the right times without burning themselves out.

Relaxed approach – Working hard can be done in a relaxed manner. Being relaxed allows successful recruitment consultants to see opportunities, solve problems, better negotiate and ultimately make more thought out decisions.

Luck – Good recruitment consultants are very lucky. Fortunately, as you'll see later in this book, you can create your own good luck.

Intuition – Top recruitment consultants follow their gut feelings about people and situations. If they feel a client is being sinister, they'll pullout. If they get a bad feeling about a candidate, they won't send them to clients.

Goal orientation – Successful recruitment consultants have goals. Their goals keep them motivated.

Passion – The most important quality of a recruitment consultant is that they're passionate about the job.

This list might seem intimidating at first, but rich recruiters don't begin the job having all of the above qualities. While some recruitment consultants may have several of these qualities naturally, or have come from a strong sales background, the majority of their skills are acquired over time. Through experience, practice, failure and success you too will develop the above qualities. You just have to put in the work and allow them time to develop.

Even passion can be developed. If you feel you're lacking passion in your current recruitment position, analyse why this is. Is it the company you work for? Is it the industry you're in? Is recruitment what you want to be doing? Try to find the cause. If recruitment is the job for you, but you're not recruiting for an industry that you're passionate about, then head towards one that you are. Then have a long term goal. Do you want to be the best recruitment consultant in your company? Do you want to be the most popular recruitment consultant in your area? Do you want to be an entrepreneur? Whatever it is, you can use your long term goal to inject passion into your recruitment role. You may have noticed I've not put "money focus" on the list above. Traditionally, hiring managers in recruitment agencies focus on hiring people who are money focused. While there's logic behind this I want to challenge this standard. It's a well-known fact that if you're to start a business it will only succeed if you're passionate about it. There's no argument there. Like any other sales position, being a recruitment consultant means you're self-employed. Yes you may work for an agency, but no one else is going to build your business for you, so you need to think like an entrepreneur. Let's take two agencies. One agency is full of money hungry recruitment consultants, the other is full of passionate recruitment consultants. If I had to invest in either of these agencies I'd put my money on the agency who hired the most passionate people. It's passion that will get you through the rejection; it's passion that will make you work a late night and it's passion that will ultimately make you money.

THE RECRUITMENT INDUSTRY

The recruitment industry can be very different between sectors. At the very top you have prestigious senior executive recruitment, and at the lower end you have recruitment for unskilled labour. However, these are subjective.

There is permanent recruitment, which is placing candidates into permanent positions. Then you have temporary recruitment, which is placing candidates into temporary positions. Recruitment consultants can work either a permanent recruitment desk, or a temporary recruitment desk. In some cases they can do both.

Some sectors are candidate led, which means candidates dictate the market. This is the case for sectors where there's a shortage of skills. Some markets are client led, which means there are more candidates than jobs, so clients can dictate who they want to hire.

The recruitment industry is notoriously difficult. If you sell products, such as laptops, they're likely to work. If they don't work you can simply exchange them for new ones with little inconvenience to your client. You can differentiate your product by improving it or modifying it to your client's needs. You certainly don't have to convince the laptop to go to your clients.

Recruitment is far more challenging than selling a product for some of the following reasons:

- You fight tooth and nail for a job and when you get one, you don't have any suitable candidates
- It's difficult to differentiate yourself from competitors
- Recruitment is a highly competitive market
- Candidates sometimes don't turn up for interviews
- Candidates don't always return your calls
- Candidates turn up late for interview
- Candidates don't always prepare for interview
- Another agency has put your candidate forward
- Client fires your candidate

- Candidate leaves the role
- Candidate tells other agencies about the role you've put them forward for
- Candidates can be demanding
- Candidates might reject the job offer
- Client might reject your candidates

As you can see, in recruitment a lot of factors are outside of your control and this is what makes it notoriously difficult. At the same time, it's also what makes it extremely fun and challenging.

Be aware of these obstacles, but don't dwell on them. Just remember that every recruiter faces these problems during their career. After reading this book, you'll be equipped with the techniques to minimise the typical challenges recruitment throws at you.

WHERE TO WORK

Working in the right industry for the right recruitment agency is essential for your success. If you're an established recruitment consultant, please feel free to skip this section.

How do you know what the right industry is for you? If you have an interest in a particular field, that's always a good start. I'm interested in finance, banking, investments and stock broking. Speaking to these types of professionals interests me, so I would work in any of these industries.

What are your interests: fashion, IT, finance, banking, engineering or a different industry? Find out and head towards that industry.

Do you want a warm desk or a cold desk? A warm desk is a desk that already has clients, this usually occurs when a recruitment consultant moves on and their desk becomes available. A cold desk is a new desk that has had no work, or little work done to it. A warm desk isn't necessarily easier, but it isn't necessarily harder either. It all depends on the work of the previous recruitment consultant. Either way you still have to work extremely hard and extremely smart.

How do you know which company to work for? Do you like working for big companies, or do you like working for smaller ones where your input is more significant? Do you want to work for a company that is very professional or more relaxed?

Other questions you may want to consider include: do I want promotion fast? Is the company doing well? (Check their turnover and profits using internet research.) What is the commission structure like? Could I open up an office for this company in a new area at some point?

Once you know the answer to these questions look at companies that recruit in your industry of interest and check out their websites to assess their values and culture. Then call and email your CV to the hiring manager and ask to meet them. To get a more experienced perspective of the company, once you've met the hiring manager ask if you can spend a day in the office to get a feel for the environment. Explain that this will benefit them as they'll be able to get a feel for you too.

You may also consider using recruitment-to-recruitment consultants, also known as a Rec2Rec, to help you find the ideal role. A Rec2Rec consultant specifically recruits recruitment consultants for recruitment companies.

If you're not in the recruitment industry yet and you're trying to break in, then you can do so by sending your CV to companies you want to work for. Follow this up with a telephone call asking them for an interview. They might say "no" at first, but keep trying by calling and asking if they'll give you an opportunity. This demonstrates the skills needed for recruitment consultancy and in the end they will find it difficult to say no.

PART 2

SELLING

WHY CLIENTS BUY FROM RECRUITERS

In my first recruitment job I was confused as to why anyone would use a recruitment company to help them hire staff. I wondered why they didn't just recruit for themselves, or ask the human resources (HR) department to do it. To help you succeed it's important to understand why clients use recruitment agencies, and appreciate how important you are.

There are several reasons why companies use recruitment agencies, including:

Expert Knowledge – As a recruitment consultant you're constantly speaking to candidates in the market. That means you know who the best people are. If a manager or an HR department recruits for themselves they know they may not be speaking to the most talented candidates out there.

Time – Whatever your client's job is, whether they're a Finance Director, an Operations Manager, etc. they'll have their day job to get on with. That means they won't have time to write job adverts, sift through hundreds of CV's, and answer inbound telephone calls from candidates. It would be more beneficial for them to hire an expert to do it for them.

Money – Your client could put an advert in a national newspaper, or put an advert online, or both, which will cost them a large amount of money. The problem here is that the adverts don't guarantee a successful candidate. Therefore, they can potentially waste a lot of money. A client doesn't pay a recruitment agency unless a candidate has been placed, so you're saving them money.

Expertise – Writing job adverts that attract the top candidates requires skill, which is gained from constantly writing job adverts. Your clients probably won't have this skill.

Cost – In some cases it is actually cheaper to hire a temporary worker and pay a recruitment company than it is to hire someone permanently.

Temporary Positions – Your client may need a temporary candidate to fill maternity leave, or long-term sickness. It is far easier to use a recruitment company in such a case.

Distressed Purchase – Your client may be short-staffed due to sickness, or employees leaving the company. In this case your client will need candidates as soon as possible to keep their business functioning.

Management – I once met a client who liked using recruitment agencies, because he didn't like managing staff. If a candidate wasn't performing he could call the recruitment agency to pull the candidate out of the job and replace them with another.

Remember how much clients need your expertise and how valuable you are.

TELEPHONE SALES

You'll spend the majority of your time on the telephone in the recruitment industry. This section explains how to sell over the telephone. I'll introduce you to the basics of telephone sales and then show you how to implement these techniques, step by step.

WHAT NOT TO DO

Let's begin with a list of what **not** to do:

Don't be over familiar

You'll naturally want to build a fast rapport with clients so you can start making money. Clients strongly dislike it when sales professionals are overly familiar without first investing time into building a relationship.

This is more easily understood if you've ever been cold called by someone you don't know and they ask questions such as: "how are you today?" or "how is the weather where you are?" While these questions may seem innocent, on the telephone they're irritating to clients when they don't know the caller. You can only ask these types of personal questions when the client knows you.

Whenever you're speaking to clients for the first few times, always keep the conversation professional and business-related.

Don't sell too soon

Imagine you and your partner have just had your third child and you're looking for a new car: a car that can seat three children, hold several prams and still have room for your shopping bags. The minute you walk into the showroom a car sales professional approaches you and tries to sell you a two-seater sports car. As beautiful as the sports car is, it's completely the opposite of what you want and need.

The problem here is that the sales professional tried to sell too soon. Instead, they should have asked insightful questions to build up their knowledge in order to guide you to your ideal vehicle.

Don't sell too soon.

Don't be pushy

Don't try to close a deal on every phone call. There's a Hollywood myth to cold calling and selling, wrongly promoting the notion that if you don't close a deal every time, you're not a good sales professional. This is simply not true. You cannot force your clients to buy your candidates if they're not recruiting. They'll simply stop taking your calls if you're too pushy.

You need to build relationships with your clients in order for them to trust you.

Don't be scared

It can be scary calling clients, especially if you're going up the hierarchy. People are generally nicer and more helpful the higher up you go. This is simply due to the fact that to manage people you need to be a good people person, so these types of people get promoted. However, this is not the case for every client and you'll encounter rudeness on occasion. Don't let this scare you, because in general people are pleasant by nature. If you act professionally, they will treat you professionally.

There is less competition at the top. Most people, including your competitors, will be too afraid to call the people high up. From a business perspective you should always aim to be where there's less competition, so don't be afraid to go right to the top. Remember, they're just people.

Don't pester your clients

While it's important to win sales and ensure your clients don't forget you, don't pester them by calling too often.

You'll present the impression that your business is not doing well if they feel you're calling too frequently. It will appear as if you're desperate for business.

I would recommend you call clients once a month. You may call more if it's necessary, for example if you're actually recruiting for them. You should also call back one week after your first introductory conversation to see if they've read the company literature you've sent them. This will speed up the process of them remembering your name.

It can be all too easy to fall into any of the traps detailed above, so be aware of them, and avoid them!

ASKING QUESTIONS

"A wise man can learn more from a foolish

question than a fool can learn from a wise
answer." - Bruce Lee

This is not as straightforward as it appears. I found this difficult initially. Some people are naturally inquisitive and ask questions with ease. I, on the other hand, would over analyse and assume I knew the answers.

"If I had an hour to solve a problem and my life depended on the answer, I would spend the first 55 minutes figuring out the proper questions to ask. For if I knew the proper questions, I could solve the problem in less than 5 minutes."– Albert Einstein

The general rule is: ask a question, and then stop talking.

With practice, questioning became a natural part of my conversation. I would recommend that you spend a great deal of time developing the art of questioning, because it is the foundation of recruitment and sales. Once you've mastered the art of questioning, recruitment will become a lot easier.

OPEN QUESTIONS

An open question is a question that cannot be answered with a simple yes or no. They encourage conversation and help to build strong relationships with your clients and candidates. They're also the questions that provide you with the most information.

An open question begins with one of the following words: Who, What, Why, Where, When and How.

Some examples include:

- How do you normally recruit?
- What recruitment agencies do you use?
- How come you favour those particular agencies?
- When is the best time to catch you on the phone?
- What qualities does your ideal candidate have?
- When did you last recruit?

If you're not yet naturally asking questions, create a question sheet, print it out and stick it where you can see it while on the telephone. At the same time, practice on your friends and family. Ask them open questions, such as:

- How was your day at work?
- How did that make you feel?
- Where did that take you?

When you practice something enough times it becomes habitual and you'll no longer need to think about it; it will happen naturally.

CLOSED QUESTIONS

A closed question is one that provokes a "yes" or "no" answer. These questions will not provide you with detailed information, but they're a powerful tool for closing and getting definite answers, for example:

- Are you the person who looks after recruitment?
- Are you happy to call me with your next vacancy?

When recruitment consultants first start it's quite common for them to ask too many closed questions. If too many closed questions are asked at the start of the telephone call it can cause the conversation to end abruptly. You should base your conversations around open questions and only use closed questions if you specifically need a "yes" or "no" answer, or to close the conversation.

EXPLORING QUESTIONS

Exploring questions are similar to open questions, but they're more focused and controlled. They start off with words such as:

- Describe
- Tell me
- Explain to me
- Give me
- Show me
- Demonstrate

For example you might ask your client to describe their perfect candidate, or describe the perfect recruitment consultant. You might ask them to explain how their recruitment process works.

ADVANCED QUESTIONING

A British psychologist called Neil Rackham developed a very powerful selling system called SPIN® selling. Rackham and his team analysed more than 35,000 sales calls made by 10,000 sales professionals in 23 countries over 12 years.

The system enables a sales professional to uncover the client's implied needs, develop these into explicit needs and then offer the client a solution to those needs. This is achieved through a sequence of four question types. This is extremely powerful for consultative selling. The four question types are as follows:

Situation Questions

Situation questions are fact-finding questions about your client's existing situation. For example:

- How big is your team?
- How often do you recruit?
- What recruitment agencies do you use?

While situation questions are an essential part of your information gathering process, they must be used wisely. Your clients will quickly become bored if you ask too many. The reason for this is that the questions only benefit you. According to Rackham, successful sales professionals ask fewer situation questions, but each one has a focus or purpose.

Problem Questions

Problem questions uncover your client's problems, dissatisfactions or difficulties. If your client doesn't have any recruitment problems then there are no grounds for your service, so these types of questions help you to identify your client's implied needs. Funnily enough Rackham found that problem questions are powerful for smaller sales, but not as effective in larger sales.

Some examples of problem questions include:

- What problems do you usually face when recruiting?

- How satisfied are you with your current recruitment agency?
- What problems would it cause you if your supplier couldn't deliver?

Implication Questions

Inexperienced recruitment consultants will usually start to sell after they've asked problem questions and identified a problem. However, this will just cause the client to raise objections. Instead, successful sales professionals and rich recruiters ask implication questions. Implication questions amplify the problem you've uncovered as it forces the client to review the effects, consequences or implications of their problems.

Some examples include:

- If your current agency's staff didn't turn up to work, how would that affect you?
- If you couldn't find a candidate with that particular skill set how would that affect your operations?
- What would happen if you didn't act on this?

Need-payoff questions

Once you've built up the client's problem so that they perceive it as more serious, you should switch to need-pay off questions, which demonstrate the value of your services. Need-payoff questions shift the focus of the client's attention off the problem and onto the solution. At the same time, the client starts telling you the benefits of your service. We discuss objection handling later in the book, but Rackham suggests that if you use need-payoff questions correctly you'll face less objections. Some examples of need-payoff questions include:

- How important is it that you solve this problem?
- If you only received a handful of relevant CV's would that help to solve your time problem?
- If you're spending that amount on job adverts with no guaranteed success, would a service where you only paid for delivered results help you?

Rackham states that SPIN® selling is "the way most successful people sell on a good day when the call is going well". You might find that you won't be able to ask all these questions in one sitting, but instead you may have to ask them in a sequence of calls over a period of time.

THE POWER OF SILENCE

You should be aware of the Pareto Principle, also known as the 80/20 Rule. This principle is named after Vilfredo Pareto, an economist who identified that 20 percent of the population owned 80 percent of the wealth. This principle is applicable to many walks of life, especially business. In business, 80 percent of your business comes from 20 percent of your clients. When selling, you should only talk 20 percent of the time while your client talks 80 percent of the time.

Your role requires you to use the telephone, but your clients and candidates should be doing most of the talking. When they talk, they reveal their buying motives.

When you've asked a question, do not feel the need to offer a selection of answers, or to answer the question for the client, for example:

"I thought you'd be interested in this candidate's CV... Or, not"

Remember the general rule is: ask a question and then stop talking. The above example would be better phrased:

"What did you think of the CV I sent you?"

If you ask a question and the client is silent, do not feel the need to fill the silence. While this is an uncomfortable situation it's an extremely powerful one, especially during a negotiation. The silence will feel longer than it actually is and your client will appreciate the time to think.

Silence is also a powerful way to get the client to expand further on their questions. This works very well in face-to-face meetings. If you want your client to keep talking after they've answered a question, remain silent and they'll immediately try and fill it with extra information.

LISTENING

Once your client begins talking and opening up to you, ensure you listen intently. This seems a simple task but many sales professionals struggle with listening. They focus so much on trying to think of what to ask next that they forget to listen to what's being said. At the same time, it can be difficult to listen when you're trying to write down what they're saying.

While it's essential that you keep the conversation going and record notes, the whole conversation is counterproductive if you're not actually listening. Worst of all, the client will know you're not listening if you ask an irrelevant question straight after they've just spoken about a different topic.

Have a list of stock questions on your desk, so that

you always have questions to ask and you don't need to worry about what to ask next. To show that you're listening, ask questions relevant to what they've just said. When you're taking notes about your client keep them short, one word per point if possible.

Whilst on the telephone it can feel awkward if the person listening is completely silent. Show the client you're still on the other end and that you're listing by making verbal confirmations, such as:

- Mmm
- Uh-huh
- Yes
- Ahhhh
- Okay
- Does that mean...
- I don't understand
- I understand

It's important that you wait until clients have finished making their point and not talk over them with your next question. It's okay to leave a short silence to ensure they've finished speaking before you begin speaking.

To help the client build confidence in you and show

them that you understand, paraphrase back to them what they've said.

FEATURES ADVANTAGES AND BENEFITS

Features, advantages and benefits, also known as FAB, is a powerful method of tailoring your sell to the client's needs.

A feature describes a characteristic of what you're selling, such as its colour, size and shape.

An advantage is what the feature does.

A benefit is how a feature meets the need expressed by your client, such as: cost saving, ease of use, safety, increased productivity and time saving. A benefit is only a benefit to your client if they've expressed a need. For example, if your client isn't looking for that particular benefit, such as ease of use, then you're actually talking about advantages. Therefore, advantages and benefits are similar, but an advantage becomes a benefit if your client explicitly expresses a particular problem. Remember the difference between the two.

If I were to sell you a pen, and explained that "it's a black inked pen", then that doesn't tell you anything useful. Only that the pen is black. However, if I know you scan a lot of your hand written documents and you suffer from many admin errors, I can use FAB to say the following: "It's a black inked pen, which means you'll be able to scan your documents more clearly resulting in less admin errors." Notice how I've discussed a feature, an advantage of that feature and the benefit to the client.

Clients buy benefits not features. While it's important to discuss the features of your product it is essential that you guide your client from features to benefits as I did in the example above.

You can do this by using connecting phrases:

- The benefit of this is...
- This means that you'll...
- As a result...

Sometimes recruitment consultants' state features, because they wrongly believe it's a benefit, or they think the client can connect the benefit to the feature. Clients can't always connect benefits to features, so be explicit with them.

To ensure you've actually got a benefit, put yourself in the client's shoes and ask yourself:

- So what?

If you can't ask "so what?", then you've drilled down enough to reach a benefit.

When selling a client a feature of one of your candidates, it could be that they're a member of a debating team. The benefit of this to your client is that they'll be able to fluently challenge senior managers during meetings. However, this is only a benefit if the client is looking for someone to challenge senior managers. Otherwise it's just an advantage.

Sometimes you'll be challenged by your prospective clients as to why they should use recruitment agencies, or even use you as a recruitment consultant. You'll need to identify the benefits for the client. Earlier in this section we identified the benefits of using a recruitment company, but what are the benefits of using specifically you?

One example could be: "We're a niche boutique recruitment agency who work with only a select few clients, which means you'll have a greater access to the best candidates."

Once you become proficient at identifying benefits for your clients, or even better getting your clients to identify the benefits of your services themselves, you'll be able to sell any product or service.

THE POWER OF THREE

There is something powerful about things in threes. The psychology of it is beyond this book, but it is believed that the human brain can only take in and analyse, efficiently, three pieces of information.

If you look around you'll see that the power of three is culturally ingrained. You'll hear politicians using it; you'll see it in the marketing of large corporations and you'll see top sales professionals using it. Some examples include:

- The three blind mice
- The three amigos
- An essay has a beginning, middle and an end
- The three wise men
- 1st 2nd 3rd
- Tony Blair's three main priorities in government were: "Education, Education, Education."
- The three R's: reading, writing and arithmetic
- Three Men and a Baby
- Small, medium and large
- Ready, aim, fire
- The Lion, the Witch and the Wardrobe

What this means is that your clients are most likely to remember the information you provide if it comes in threes. Have you ever been on the telephone to a sales professional and they tell you so much information that by the fifth point you can't remember the detail of the earlier points? Have you ever asked someone for directions and after they give you the third road or direction, you just can't remember?

Keep your information in three succinct points. Now we can take this further and combine the power of three with benefits. By selling to your client using three benefits you'll be delivering an extremely influential pitch that they can, and will, remember.

Whether you're selling over the telephone, through an email, face-to-face or through a presentation, use the power of three to organise the structure of your sell. Break it into three parts: an introduction, middle and an end. I recommend that you also write your job adverts, e-shots and conduct your interviews with this same structure, which I'll demonstrate in later sections.

LEARN TO ASK

"How come you're not getting any meetings with clients?"

"I'm not sure."

"Are you asking for meetings?"

"No, I guess not."

"Start asking for them!"

One month later I had meetings with Finance Directors of some very well-known companies. By the end of my first year I had met with 90% of the clients on my patch. I'll show you in a later chapter how to book meetings, but first I want to highlight the importance of asking for something.

"If you don't ask, you don't get." - Mahatma Gandhi

If you want something in life you have to ask for it. If you want your clients to use your services as a recruitment consultant, you'll have to ask them to. If you want a pay rise, or you want to expand your recruitment desk into a new market then you'll have to ask your boss.

"If you don't ask, the answer is always no." - Nora Roberts

Depending on how assertive you are, asking for things can be quite scary, especially if you're afraid of rejection. As Nora Roberts said, if you don't ask the answer will always be no. That means if you don't ask clients for meetings, or for their business they won't give it to you.

Practice asking your clients for things, such as:

- Can I recruit for your next vacancy?
- Can I come and meet you?
- Can I have your direct telephone line? I promise not to abuse it.
- Can I have your email address?

Taking this beyond recruitment you'll be amazed at what you get in life if you ask for it. I encourage you to do this outside of work. If you're in a restaurant ask for a free side plate of chips, or ten percent off the bill. Ask someone you find attractive for their telephone number. Ask someone you admire if they will mentor you, or go to dinner and share their knowledge with you. You might read this and think "I can't possibly do that". If you don't ask, the answer will always be "no" and you won't get anything.

The odds are stacked in your favour. If you get an "OK" you've achieved your goal, if you get a "no" then you've lost nothing.

CLOSING

Leading on from the last section is the art of closing. I must make a clear difference between closing and closing techniques. Closing is when you get a commitment from your client so that the relationship progresses to the next stage. For example, this could be a meeting with your client, or the client giving you a vacancy to fill. Closing doesn't always mean closing a sale, which it's more commonly known for. Closing techniques are techniques that help you reach a close. As I mentioned earlier closing is usually associated with closing the sale, but this is now very old school thinking and in today's world you won't be using these traditional closing techniques to close the sale. Instead you'll use them to close stages that progress the client forward, for example a meeting. I'll show you how to book meetings with clients later in the book.

Closing is notoriously difficult for sales professionals most probably because it can feel rude and awkward. It also sets you up for the possibility of being rejected. There are usually two extremes: one, when the sales professional tries to close too soon and close too much, making the client feel pressured; the second extreme is when the sales professional won't close, which makes the client feel irritated.

Returning to Neil Rackham's research, he found that when selling low value goods an increased use of closing made more sales. However, in high value goods an increased use of closing decreased the chances of making a sale. In other words, closing techniques become less effective as decision size increases.

There is a famous saying in sales: "always be closing", also known as ABC. This is very outdated and wrong in recruitment. If you try to close your clients from the start they'll feel pushed into something they don't want, or something they're not ready for yet. The idea is to guide your clients not push them. Instead of "always be closing" think "always be consulting."

There is no mysterious secret to closing other than asking your client for some commitment and then staying quiet until your client speaks first.

Traditional Closing Techniques

There are several different types of closing techniques, which work well in the initial stages of winning a client, such as getting a meeting or the client giving you a vacancy to fill. However, these techniques work less well when closing a sale. Winning a client and winning a sale are two very distinct scenarios in certain recruitment sectors. For example, you may win the opportunity to recruit for your client, but it doesn't mean your candidate will get the job at the end of the recruitment process. At this point you've won the client but you've not made a sale. However, in other recruitment sectors, such as industrial recruitment, winning the client usually means winning the sale because you become the sole recruiter for that client. For simplicity, this book separates the two.

The following closing techniques can be used over the telephone or face-to-face.

Gentle close:

- Do you feel that we could help you recruit?
- Do you feel a meeting would benefit you?

This is a gentle close because it's nonthreatening and the client won't feel pushed. It allows your client to either say "yes", or come up with a reservation. If the client comes back with a reservation, you then go back to consulting and questioning.

Alternative close:

- I'm in your area on the 18th and 21st, are you around for a quick meeting?

In this close you're asking them to choose between two alternative options.

Assumptive close:

- This looks good to me. I can get CV's to you by the end of the week.
- You probably want to get started on this now.
- So you'll call me for your next vacancy?

This type of close assumes that the client wants to progress forward with you.

Conditional close:

- If I can work at 19% would you be happy for me to work on this vacancy?

This close is best when your client has one condition that they can only work to, such as a limited budget.

Invitational close:

- Why don't you try me for one vacancy and if you like the CV's I send you, you can look at taking things forward?
- Why don't you just let me send you one CV to benchmark it against your preferred suppliers?

This close invites the client to test your services with no long-term commitment or risk.

Empathy close:

- I'm confident that I can recruit the right person for you based on everything I know. What else do I need to do in order for us to work together?
- Some of my best clients have "felt" the same way. That was until I sent them some CV's and they met my candidates.

This close takes into account the feelings of the client and demonstrates that you understand them.

Puppy dog close:

- "Why don't you try my candidate for a day? We won't charge you, and you'll be able to see if they're the right fit for your department?"

The puppy dog close comes from pet shops when customers are hesitating over buying a puppy. The shop keeper lets the customer take the puppy home for the night and if they change their mind they can bring the puppy back the next day. The seller knows once the customer takes the puppy home they'll never be able to bring it back, which closes the sale.

You can use these types of closing techniques to move the client forward. Remember, if the client says "no", that just means "not right now". Remain relaxed and confident and the client will believe in you.

When To Close

You must close otherwise it will irritate your client until they become so impatient they leave the telephone call. For example:

Consultant: "What else do you need to know?"

Client: "Nothing, I think you've covered everything."

Consultant: "Great, are you sure I can't go through anything else with you?"

Client: "No, honestly, but now I've got to go."

Consultant: (*desperate*) "But we've gone through everything?"

In the example above the recruitment consultant doesn't know how to draw the conversation to an end, so the client leaves. As you can see the idea is to close, but the key is to close at the right time. If you never close the client will leave irritated, but if you try to close too early the client will feel pressured.

Therefore, you need to ensure the client is happy to move forward. Take the following example:

Consultant: (assumptive close) "I'm glad you liked the CV's, I'll arrange interviews for you over the next few weeks?"

Client: "Wow, hold on, what's your rebate period."

Consultant: (alternative close) "I'll send you our terms of business, which contains the rebate period, so can you do interviews this Tuesday or Thursday?"

Client: (pressured) "Hold on, what are you covering up?"

It's obvious in this example that the client becomes irritated when they're not ready to move forward and the recruitment consultant tries to close. This makes the recruitment consultant look pushy and sinister. A rich recruiter would check to see if the client is happy first before trying to move the client forward. For example:

Consultant: "It looks like we've covered everything. Can I check you're happy with everything, or do you have any reservations?"

Client: "Yes, you haven't mentioned your rebate period."

Consultant: "I'll tell you about that now. If you've not satisfied with your candidate you can have a full refund after one month, but this decreases by 50% after two months..."

So when exactly is the right time to close? As the conversation draws to a conclusion and the client has no reservations then you should summarise the client's problems and your benefits, which will then be followed by your close. For example:

Consultant: "It looks like we've covered everything. Can I check you're happy with everything, or do you have any reservations? "

Client: "No, that's everything."

Consultant: (summary) "So your current supplier isn't providing you with the quality of candidates you need. As a result, you're short staffed, so your team is working overtime. I can certainly help you with this as I have access to a greater pool of candidates."

Client: "Yes, that sounds good."

Consultant: (closing) "Then the next logical step would be to take a job specification and provide you with some CVs?"

The next step will depend on your client's situation. If they're not currently recruiting, the next step might be a face-to-face meeting. Notice how the conversation has naturally progressed to the close rather than forcing a close. Also notice that the rich recruiter hasn't asked, but instead told the client what the next logical step is. This is extremely important in closing.

Closing The Sale

In the above section I discussed closing to progress the client forward. This could be a meeting, or taking a job specification. Notice how I've not discussed closing the sale. In recruitment, closing techniques are best used to progress the client towards the sale, but not for closing the sale. This is because closing techniques aren't required when the client wants to buy. If your client is recruiting, and you provide the best candidate, they'll want to hire them, so you simply won't need to close.

If your candidate isn't the best person for the job, there's no closing technique in the world that will get your client to buy. If somehow you did manage to pressure your client into hiring the wrong candidate, this would be a guaranteed way to destroy any future business with them.

In summary, use closing techniques only to progress the client forward. The close will come naturally as you ask the right questions, but you must close otherwise no progression will be made. To close, firstly, check to see if the client has any reservations. Secondly, summarise what they've told you and explain the benefits. Lastly, close by telling the client what the next logical step is. In the later stages of the recruitment process, when the client wants to buy, you won't need closing techniques.

OPENING A SALES CALL

Whether you're opening the call for the first time or the tenth time, always:

- Introduce yourself using both first name and surname
- State what company you're calling from
- State why you're calling
- Ask for permission to continue. The permission to continue might be to ask questions or ask if they're free to speak

From a very young age most of us are taught not to speak to strangers and that strangers are bad. Even as we grow into adults we carry these negative associations with us. Therefore, it's important to introduce yourself upfront so you're not seen as a complete stranger. Even on the tenth or twentieth call you should open your calls in such a structured way.

BODY LANGUAGE FOR TELEPHONE SALES

"It's not what you say, but how you say it." - Anon

When you're on the telephone to your friends and family you know if they're lying down or rushing from one location to the next without even having to ask them. You can tell if they're happy, sad, worried, anxious, excited, in a rush or ecstatic. You know this because the sound, pitch and tone of their voice are different depending on their activity and mood.

People become more aware of how you're speaking when you're on the telephone. The reason for this, I can imagine, is that their hearing and imagination becomes heightened by the absence of your physical presence. Therefore, if you slouch in your chair during your telephone calls your body will feel too relaxed. The sound of your voice will change due to the physical structure of your body being in a more crunched up position. If you were to say a power-ful phrase, such as: "I'm enthusiastic to work with you. You can be confident that I'd find you the right candidate," but you said it from a slouched position, your client will not feel your enthusiasm or your capability. If this was your first telephone call to a client this would be their first impression of you.

Although you're on the telephone, and your clients can't physically see you, they visualise you by your voice. Therefore, your body language needs to be in a strong and dynamic position. Sit up in your chair with your back straight and your head up. This posture opens up your throat and stomach making you sound clearer, articulate, confident and professional.

If you have a difficult client or an important tele-phone call, stand up and walk around during the call. You'll feel more powerful and this will transfer into your voice. Most importantly, find a style that suits your personality.

DEALING WITH REJECTION

While in the office have you ever been offered a drink when you're not thirsty, and replied "No, thank you"? Were you rejecting the person or the drink? Have you ever offered a drink to someone in the office and they said "No, thank you?" Did you feel rejected? Probably not because you accept they're not thirsty, just as you're not thirsty sometimes.

There are times when your client isn't recruiting for whatever reason and they say "no" to you. It's important not to take it personally. They're not rejecting you or your candidate for any other reason other than the fact that they're not recruiting at that point in time.

More experienced recruitment consultants understand this and they realise "no" really means "not right now". At some point in the future, your client will be recruiting and they will need your services. What determines your success is whether you have the ability to keep calling back. Eventually you'll call at the right time, send an e-shot at the right time, or build such a good relationship that they call you.

In a way it's that simple, but from experience I know how mentally difficult the job can actually be. I've been there when every telephone call is followed by another "no". It can be demoralising and you can start to question whether it is your ability as a recruitment consultant. Remember that it's not you, or your ability.

How you see rejection is largely down to your mentality and life experiences. Top recruitment consultants know they're not going to be successful 100 percent of the time. Instead they see it as a challenge. Winning first place in a competition, a football game, or any type of event is only rewarding if you've had to work hard for it. It says you've had to fight and crawl through fire to get there. Top recruitment consultants love to hear "no", because they love the challenge of turning it into a "yes".

In fact you can only begin selling once you hear "no". You're in consultative sales not transactional sales. You're paid to turn a "no" into a "yes". If you wanted it to be that easy you'd get a transactional sales job where customers came to you.

There are techniques to help you with any mental barriers you're facing. Try to turn it into a game and see how many clients you can get to say "no" before you get a "yes". If you're new to recruitment, jump in the deep end and face your fears by making as many calls as you can. The best way to conquer your fear is to face it head on. Once you've had a few rejections the impact will be less mentally draining, as your mind adapts to your environment.

See rejection as a good thing, because it'll make you a stronger person. I sat next to a colleague, who was on a particularly easy patch. Every day she would get a job from her marketing activities. Eventually she left her job for a different company for several months, but then came back. When she came back she was placed on a different patch. Unfortunately, she wasn't mentally prepared for the difficulties of a different economic patch and she couldn't handle the constant rejection. If she had begun her career on a difficult patch where she had to face constant rejection before the clients would accept her, she would have built up the mental resistance against rejection.

Colonel Sanders, the founder of Kentucky Fried Chicken (KFC) was turned down 1000 times before he got a "yes". In recruitment you may hear "no" more than 1000 times before you get a "yes". I did, so don't let it knock you.

Return to this section often to reconfirm you're doing your job well. Realise that you're good at your job and eventually the hard work will pay off. Keep telling yourself this every day.

PRACTICE MAKES PERFECT

Your muscles and brain grow accustomed to repetitive actions until you no longer have to think before you do it. This is well known in professional sport and it's why for a 48 minute boxing match, a 60 minute football game, or a two minute gymnastics routine alike, hundreds of hours of repetitive practice and training are dedicated to perfection. It is simply not enough to read about it, you have to practice it over and over again until it becomes a natural reaction.

Sales and recruitment is no different. You'll find that when you start the job and a client throws an objection your way, you'll stumble and stutter over your words as you 'find' the answer in your head, or around your desk if you've pinned up a list of answers. However, over time you won't even need to think and your telephone calls and objection handling will flow naturally.

This will happen with experience, but you can speed up the learning process through practice and role-playing. To practice questioning, ask your family and friends open questions about their day and life, such as: "How was your day today?"

Ask a colleague or your manager if they'll spend some time with you at the start of the day to role-play objection handling. Also ask them to help you role-play sales meetings and delivering sales presentations.

If you want to go a step further, take a short course in acting and public speaking. Standing in front of an audience acting and improvising lines helps you to become confident while enabling you to think on your feet. Improvising refers to when actors are not given a script and they must make it up on the spot, or they forget their lines and improvise. Acting classes are relatively cheap and the return on investment is worth every penny. Not only will your sales skills increase, but you'll have fun, meet new friends and learn new skills.

GETTING PAST GATEKEEPERS

"You shall not pass!" – Gandalf the Grey

The term gatekeepers refers to the people who act as barriers between you and your client. They can be receptionists, personal assistants or anyone who generally looks after inbound telephone calls.

Part of their job is to prevent, or limit, contact between you and the client. Not all companies treat inbound calls the same. Some have switchboards that'll put you straight through without any hassle. Others will have Spartan like gatekeepers who will block your every advancement.

SHOW RESPECT

The first rule is: treat gatekeepers with the highest

respect. They're people who are doing a job just as you're doing yours. It can be frustrating at times, and yes, some gatekeepers can be unfriendly. However, don't take it personally. They're constantly answering the phone at what I can imagine to be a very tedious job. They may be having a bad day and unintentionally direct their frustration at you. If you're ever rude to a gatekeeper they will simply tell their boss never to do business with you. Always treat gatekeepers how you would expect to be treated.

KNOW THE CLIENT'S NAME

Gatekeepers are unlikely to put you through to the client if you don't know the name of the client, so asking for the Director is going to get you the response: "They're in a meeting". If you want to increase your chances of being put through to the client you'll need to know their name. Asking for the client by name gives the impression that you know them, so the gatekeeper will check to see if they're available for you.

What if you don't know their name? Use the internet to find the name of the client you're after. You can do this by putting into an internet search engine the name of the company and the job title of the person you're looking for. I strongly suggest that you use LinkedIn to find and connect with people you want to do business with.

What if that doesn't come up with anything? While gatekeepers will try and prevent you from speaking with clients they won't, usually, withhold the names of clients. You can phone the switchboard and ask for the name of the Director or whatever their job title is. Only in some companies will the gatekeeper not provide this information, but this is rare. They might not give you an email address, but they'll see no harm in giving you a name. You'll need to be very polite and humble. If you call and demand the name of the client you'll get a dial tone in return. To win the gatekeeper over be polite and ask for help, people love helping people. For example you might say.

You: "Hello, my name is <name> and I'm calling from <your company>, I was wondering if you could help me, please?"

Gatekeeper: "Okay."

You: "I'm after the name of your Finance Director, Please."

Gatekeeper: "Sure it's Susan Smith."

You: "Thank you so much."

If the gatekeeper gives you the client's name, always ask for more, like we discussed earlier.

You: "Could I send them an email please?"

Gatekeeper: "Yes, it's susan.smith@remember_to_ ask.com."

You: "Thank you so much."

Can you ask for the name of the client and then ask to be put through? Yes, but usually gatekeepers won't put you through on this occasion, but do try anyway. While they'll be happy to supply you with the name they might not put you through, because they know you don't know the client. However, now that you have the name of the client you can basically phone back in the next couple of days.

The gatekeeper heard 'recruitment' and won't give you the name of the client? Arnold Schwarzenegger once gave a speech about how he reached success. He described six rules for success. One of his rules was that you've got to break the rules. Translating this to your situation, if the gatekeeper won't give you the information and you can't find anything on the internet, then you've got to think creatively and problem solve. I've heard top recruitment consultants calling gatekeepers and pretending to be calling from fictitious trade magazines. They then ask the gatekeeper for the name and email address of the client, so they can send them a free copy of the magazine. Some have called up saying they were a student and wanted to send the client an email to help with their studies. I'm not familiar with all the laws and regulations across different countries, but if you know the laws and rules then you can learn to bend them without breaking them. So what other creative ways can you think of for getting the name of the gatekeeper?

GETTING DIRECT TELEPHONE LINES

You know the name of the client, but the gatekeeper still won't put you through? Occasionally you can be faced with companies that won't put any sales calls through. Usually clients have direct lines, and these can be a variation of the main company number. When calling sometimes you'll be asked if you know the extension via an automated switchboard, or in some cases you can simply just dial the direct number and go straight to the client. If you know direct numbers you can then cut straight past the gatekeeper. If you don't have the direct number of your client there are creative ways to acquire it.

If you have the direct number of anyone else in the company you can call them and play dumb.

Katie: "Hello."

You: "Is that Susan Smith?"

Katie: "No, she's on 245."

You: "Sorry my mistake."

Now you have your client's extension number.

What if you don't have anyone's direct number? Try changing the last digit or the last few digits of the company's telephone number to see if that puts you through. If that doesn't work, it's a waiting game until an opportunity arises. However, you can help opportunities happen and I'll show you how.

Many people assign a signature to the bottom of their emails containing their direct number and mobile number. You'll need the client to email you so you can see the signature and capture their information. If you send a generic e-shot or an introductory email and the client isn't recruiting they're unlikely to reply. If you send an insightful email with an interesting question they're more likely to reply. Now you need to find a reason to email. Check the business sections of local newspapers or online news to see if the company has any good stories. If so send a 'well done' email to the client along with a question that causes them to reply. You could send this from your work email to try and start the working relationship. If you think the client won't take the bait, because you're a recruitment consultant, send the email as a civilian from a public email account, such as Hotmail or Google Mail. You could even set up a public email account just for these particular activities. An example could be:

"Hi Susan,

We've not spoken before. My name is <name> a student from a local university. I recently read in the news that your company has received an award for being a good employer to work for.

I'm sorry to trouble you, but I was wondering if you could help me, please? I am writing a dissertation about employee engagement and would relish the opportunity to hear what your top three tips are for creating such a successful working environment?

Kind regards,

<name (but not your name)>"

Most people would reply to such an email, because people are naturally programmed to help other people. It would also appeal to their ego as you've specifically asked them. Notice in the email I've asked for help and I've kept it very short. Also remember not to use your personal email or your personal name. You could always ask a friend or family member to do this for you. This requires a lot of thought and preparation so I wouldn't advise you do this for every client. I would use this technique if I couldn't get past a gatekeeper and had tried many times.

Around the holiday periods such as the summer you'll find that many emails or e-shots that you send will probably be returned with an automatic 'out of office' reply. This automatic reply may have a signature at the bottom, which you can use to acquire their information. At the same time they usually write an out of office message along the lines of:

> *"I am currently out of office until xx/xx/xx in case of an emergency you can contact me on <mobile number> or call Timothy Burns on <direct line>. I will reply to you when I get back to the office."*

Now you have their mobile number and a second contact to call with their direct line, great. Please do not call your client's mobile while they're on annual leave, you'll probably get an unpleasant response.

If I telephone call for a client and I've been informed they're on holiday I'll immediately send them a blank anonymous email from a disposable temporary email address such as Guerrilla Mail to catch any out of office replies. You can use Guerrilla Mail by visiting www.guerrillamail.com.

Another method to get your client's details is to keep an eye out for any candidates on the market who have worked for your client. Then ask them for reference details and they should supply you with the relevant information.

While you're waiting for these opportunities to arise, you can still be proactive. Try calling at different times. Your client might start work early and work late when the gatekeeper isn't around. Therefore, any telephone calls before 9am and after 5pm might get through to the client. If you have a specifically difficult gatekeeper, keep trying regardless. One day they'll be on leave and their replacement may be less experienced or less difficult.

Try and become friendly with gatekeepers and personal assistants, get them on your side by taking an interest in them. To do this, ask them questions about their work and life. A client is more likely to do business with you if their personal assistant tells them to give you a chance. In some cases the personal assistant vets the email box of their boss, so they'll ensure your email gets through if they like you.

THANK YOU METHOD

Another method available is the "thank you" method. I personally don't like this method, because it doesn't fit with my personality. However, it might work for you and it's another tool for you to try. The thank you method is based around an assertive instruction rather than asking for permission. It goes like this:

You: "Hello, Susan Smith, thank you."

Gatekeeper: "Who's calling, please?"

You: "< your name>, thank you."

Gatekeeper: "Where are you calling from?"

You: "<your company>, thank you."

Gatekeeper: "Thank you, putting you through."

Notice you're not asking for permission, instead

you're giving the gatekeeper an instruction. It also gives the impression that you've spoken to the client before.

CALL SECURITY

Gatekeepers are trained to ask the client if they're free to speak before putting you through. This gives the client the opportunity to say "no", so the gatekeeper will return to you and tell you the client is busy or in a meeting. However, security will generally put you through without asking your client. When I have difficulty getting hold of a client I call the security desk. I explain I've phoned them by accident and ask if they could put me through to the name of client, which they usually do.

Above are a variety of methods to get past the gatekeeper, what other methods can you think of?

GETTING CLIENT'S EMAILS

When you first speak to a client you should always ask them for their email address. However, it can be hard to obtain an email address if you can't get your client on the telephone and the receptionist won't hand it out.

If you send charming emails or powerful e-shots, clients will usually get back to you for your services, so acquiring their email is important.

There are several ways to acquire your client's email address. The first method is simply to ask the gatekeeper for it. Usually they'll give it to you, but there'll be occasions when the company has a policy of not handing out email addresses. We like a challenge!

If you're trying to speak to a client but you're faced with a gatekeeper who's following the company's 'no sales call' policy, try doing an internet search on your client. If you know the name of the person you're trying to reach, type in a search engine their name followed by the '@' symbol followed by the company's website domain name. For example: "Andrew + @therichrecruiter.com" and check at least five pages that the search engine produces. Using this method I've found direct numbers and email addresses from company PDFs and Word documents that are floating on the internet. Even if you don't know the name of the client you can still perform this type of search. Simply search for the job title instead. For example: "Finance Director + @ therichrecruiter.com". Also try "email + @clientsdomainname.com".

Another way is to do research on other employees in the company to see if you can find their email address. Someone in marketing may have done an event and their email address is in the public domain, which might look like this:

david.williams@company.com

Using this email address you now know what the company's email address format is, which in this case is:

firstname.surname@company.com

Using this format you can now work out the email address of your prospective client.

You can also try to guess their email by taking their website domain and trying variations of the client's name, for example:

andrewleong@companyname.com
andrew.leong@companyname.com
leong@companyname.com
andrew@companyname.com
andrewl@companyname.com
al@companyname.com
aleong@companyname.com
a.leong@companyname.com
leong.a@companyname.com

Now combine your guesses with an online email

verifier such as: 'mailtester.com' and it'll tell you if you've guessed correctly.

Most medium to large sized companies have a buying or procurement department. The job of buyers and procurement specialists is to interact with sales professionals, review suppliers, save costs and improve quality. They expect to be called by sales professionals and will hand out their email address so you can provide them with more information. Typically, gatekeepers will put sales professionals through to the procurement and buying departments without objection.

Now this is the interesting part. Unless you recruit for buyers and procurement employees then the person you're speaking to in procurement isn't your prospect client. However, the objective is to acquire their email address and learn the format of the company's email addresses. Ask for the email address of the person you're speaking to in procurement and they'll give it to you.

If you feel uncomfortable telephoning the procurement department as a recruitment consultant who recruits for an unrelated area, there's an alternative approach. I've seen rich recruiters call up procurement and say they're calling from a fictitious company who makes printers, stationery or anything that the company may buy and ask for the procurement person's email address.

There'll be times when you're faced with a brick wall and you can't get any information that'll help you get in touch with your client. In this case try networking events and seeking out people who could put you in contact with your prospect client. Remember, you'll have to also add value to the networking group and help the networkers who've helped you. If you're an international recruiter a local networking event may not have any potential for you. Instead try LinkedIn and see if you and your prospective client have any mutual connections. Then ask your mutual connection to introduce you to your prospective client.

If you recruit for your local patch try running your own networking events. This way you can invite your target market and you'll be seen as a key person of influence. In the situation where you cannot get in contact with a prospective client, use the networking event to invite someone else from their organisation. Then build a relationship up with them and ask them to introduce you to your prospective client.

As you've seen in this section, there are numerous ways of getting what you want simply by asking.

However, if you come up against objections or obstacles think of ways around them. Never take "no" as a permanent answer.

FINDING CLIENTS

You may have started recruitment on a warm desk or a cold desk. You may at some point change jobs or be asked to start a new desk in a new industry. Whatever your situation, you'll have to know how to find new clients. Even if you have an established desk, the business world is always changing. People change jobs, companies go bust, new companies are created and some companies are relocated. This means your patch is constantly changing. In this section I'll show you how to find companies and clients.

CANDIDATE INTELLIGENCE

When you register candidates for your recruitment agency, check to see if they're a client or a potential client. It's common for candidates to become clients and clients to become candidates. Identity whether the company they work for, or have worked for, is on your patch. Ask them for references that you can contact. A reference is a great reason to contact your client.

Candidates can give you a wealth of information about your target client and their department. They'll know if you're trying to interrogate them or use them in any way, so you'll need to be subtle in your approach. Ask them subtle questions such as what software systems they used, who they managed and who they reported to. These questions help you understand their role more, but they also help you to understand the department of the company you're targeting.

DRIVE ROUND

After visiting clients, take some time to drive round the area and look at surrounding companies. There could be other companies worth marketing. Look out for commercial vehicles and advertising boards for any companies that may need your recruitment services.

If you're driving, have a colleague write down the names of the companies for you. If you're alone, use an audio recording device such as a Dictaphone and say the names of the companies. When you get back to the office you can use the internet to find the contact details of any potential clients within those companies. Keep the audio file or paper you wrote the names of the companies on for your manager. They may want to know why you spent so much time on your client meeting.

If you're ambitious you can do a drive round in your spare time. If you're in a situation where you can't do a drive round, use Google Maps street view to do a virtual drive round.

BUSINESS DIRECTORIES

Check business directories both online and offline for companies that could use recruitment services on your patch.

When working a particular patch, I like to get a list of all companies in that area and go through each one to see if they're worth putting on my marketing list.

LINKEDIN

LinkedIn is a quick and easy way to find new clients on your patch. When logged into LinkedIn, go to a search engine, such as Google, and type in:

"LinkedIn + Area + Job Title" – (replace area with your patch area and job title for the position that your client would hold).

Then press 'enter'. This should bring up results of

people in your area with that job title. Add their details to your client database and mark them as your target market.

We will discuss LinkedIn in more detail later in the book, and how to do more advanced searches.

NEWSPAPERS

Read local newspapers and online news every morning to identify any new businesses that have been set up on your patch. Reading local news is also a good way of identifying any change that is happening. For example, if you read that a company has announced redundancies this is an opportunity to call and help your client. Your client and their staff will need help with CV's and registering with an agency. If your client has been lucky enough to keep their job but has lost staff, they may need temporary staff to cover work load.

I read in the paper that a well-known retail company that specialised in sports clothing had gone into administration. I was already aware of this possibly happening from speaking to my clients within the company, but I found out through the newspaper. As soon as I found out, I telephoned the Finance Director and asked if he would like me to register him and his team. He welcomed the idea and I spent the day at their head office recruiting some fantastic candidates. I managed to place some of the candidates while the rest got jobs in other big companies outside of my patch. They remembered everything I did for them.

The news doesn't have to be a negative change. I read that a large manufacturing company was doing amazingly well on my patch. As a result, I knew they'd need extra staff. At the same time I knew all their suppliers on my patch would be doing well too as they tried to keep up with demand. In this case the suppliers were so unprepared for the demand that their staff had to work long, gruelling hours, which caused high staff turnover. When I was calling these clients they not only need more staff, but they were asking to meet with me so I could register them as candidates.

WHO ELSE SHOULD YOU BE SPEAKING TO?

You can have multiple clients within a company, and once you have earned the trust of your client it is fine to ask:

- Who else should I be speaking to within your company?

You might be speaking to the top person, but the mangers below them may be in charge of their own recruitment. You might be speaking to a manager who has someone above them, or a colleague next to them who uses recruitment companies. Keep asking questions and keep asking for things.

RELATIONSHIP BUILDING

A large part of selling is about building relationships with your clients. The overall reason for this is so they approach you for their recruitment needs. I've seen many sales professionals get this part wrong, not only in recruitment but in many sales professions. This is because they misunderstand the term 'relationship', and mistake it for "friendship". While it's not uncommon for your clients to become friends this isn't your overall goal and it's not what you should be aiming for. So what does relationship mean in sales? Relationship in sales means that clients perceive you as the best person for the job. It means they come to you and buy from you because you supply them with the right service at the right time.

Another mistake I've seen many recruitment consultants make is mistreating candidates. Remember your clients and candidates are the same thing. It's a small world and you'll be working with the same clients and candidates on a daily basis for many years. They'll be talking about you with each other, so they'll either be saying you're great, or advising each other to stay away from you.

There are ways to help build and secure long-term relationships with both your clients and your candidates, which we'll go through in this section. Firstly, let's identify what *not* to do. Ensure you *don't* do the following things:

1. Increase your fee rate once the client wants your candidate
2. Cancel a meeting last minute with either a client or candidate
3. Communicate poorly with either a client or candidate
4. Be over familiar
5. Be sleazy
6. Over promise and under deliver
7. Try to make the client your best friend

Now we can concentrate on what *to* do to build strong relationships with both your clients and your candidates.

STICK TO BUSINESS

There are mixed feelings about discussing personal

interests and family life with clients. Some sales experts believe you should build rapport by finding common ground, so you should seek to talk about personal interests and family. The psychology behind this is that people like to associate with like-minded people. Therefore, they're more likely to buy from you if they think you're the same. On the other side, sales experts say you should stick to business matter only. So who's right?

They're both right, but you should only ever start to get personal after a sale has been made. Until a sale has been made you should spend all of your time demonstrating what a high class professional recruiter you are, which means sticking to business matters. Now hang on, don't you need to get personal and build a relationship to make a sale? Don't fall into the trap of trying to make the client your best friend. Especially avoid this on the first telephone call. A relationship isn't built by knowing the details of your client's personal life. It's built by knowing the details of their business and their recruitment problems. Once you get the sale, then you can start to ask the client more personal questions. Until then, keep it 100 percent professional. Now I know many recruiters, especially old school recruiters, will disagree with this advice; so let's look at it in another way. Imagine you're recruiting for a position and you have two recruitment consultants on the job for you. Do you take the candidate that's best for your business? Or do you take the candidate from the recruitment consultant who knows the details of your personal life? Obviously you would take the best candidate for your business.

Now at the same time, you must consider your industry, the culture of the country your client lives in and the personality of the client. Consequently, some research is required by you to understand your market. However, if you're recruiting in the UK or America, stick to business. You may let the client take the lead on personal interests and if they go down a more personal route then you can follow, but make sure you don't go off topic too much. If your client starts talking about fishing and you consequently spend an hour on the telephone talking about fishing, while this may appear to be a great rapport building conversation, it's not. Your focus needs to be on their recruitment issues and how you can help. At the same time, spending an hour on the telephone talking about non-business related issues makes you lose credibility. A rich recruiter is a key influencer whose time is precious and respected. You certainly don't have time to talk about unrelated matters.

If your client starts taking you off topic you can bring it back using the following technique.

Client: "I've spent the weekend fishing".

You: "I would love to try fishing it looks like such a fun hobby. While I've got you on the telephone, I just want to run a candidate past you…"

BUILDING TRUST

If a client is to do business with you they must trust you. If a candidate is going to let you help find them a new role they must also trust you. Now you can't say "Just trust me," and everyone will trust you. You have to demonstrate you're a trustworthy person. There are several ways to build trust:

1. Don't sell them irrelevant candidates
2. Don't be pushy
3. Listen to them
4. If they tell you information is confidential treat it confidentially
5. Don't gossip to candidates or clients
6. Never talk badly about your competitors
7. Be friendly and pleasant
8. Do what you promise to do at the time you promised
9. Keep in touch

It's that simple.

SPEAK POSITIVELY

Words are extremely powerful, so powerful they can break hearts or inspire a nation.

Speaking positively will not only make you feel good, but it'll make the recipient feel good too. If you have a friend who's positive I bet you always look forward to speaking to them. This is how you want your clients to feel about you.

COMPLIMENTS

I've heard many sales professionals use compliments to try and build rapport with prospect clients. It seems quite reasonable, because a compliment makes you feel good. The trap with compliments is that they have the opposite effect if the receiver believes you're after something in return. Every buyer knows that a sales professional is after a sale, so that means any compliment can be received negatively. It is also creepy if the client doesn't know you well enough.

I never realised how sleazy a compliment sounded until I was called by a salesman. He called me and said: "You're Andrew, right? I saw your picture on the company website. You're a good looking guy." Now apart from thinking he's an absolute liar, it was also weird.

I advise you to keep it professional and leave compliments aside. The only exception being what Leil Lowndes, in her book *How To Talk To Anyone*, calls carrier pigeon kudos. This is a compliment from another person, which you have simply passed on. For example

You: "I was speaking to a previous employee of yours the other day, Dave Jones. He said what a good manager you are and how much you taught him."

As this is a compliment that's only being passed on by you, it avoids the negative effects of a direct compliment. Therefore it's seen positively. However, don't make these up, only use them if they're truthful and don't use them all the time on the same client. Compliments are like diamonds, if they're rare they're precious.

BUILDING CONFIDENCE

Building confidence means that clients believe that you can do the job and that they feel safe in your hands. It also means candidates will feel the same way about you finding them a job. Confidence does take time to build, but you can certainly speed up the process. Here are some examples:

Only speak to the client about relevant candidates:

If you only speak to clients about relevant candidates their confidence in you will increase, as they see that you understand their business. The same applies to candidates, if you run roles past them that are relevant their confidence will grow too.

Under promise and over deliver:

Your clients will expect you to move mountains to find the best candidates and they'll expect it at lightning speed. Your candidates will expect you to find them a new role with the same expectations. You'll want to come across as an expert recruitment consultant without setting their standards too high. The best way to do this is to carefully manage everyone's expectations. There's a well-known sales phrase I like, which goes: "Under promise over deliver". If your client gives you a vacancy to fill, don't say "No problem I'll get you the perfect candidate by the end of the day", because you're setting yourself up for a fall. If you're given a difficult role to recruit it's better to say something like: "The candidate availability for this role is quite short at the moment, I'll see what I can do, but I can't promise anything".

Do as you promised:

Breaking a promise is a confidence breaker. In business, while you might not say the words "I promise", every commitment you make is seen as a promise. If you tell a client or a candidate that you'll call them, you must call them at the exact time you said you would.

Testimonials and recommendations:

What if I told you that you could build trust and confidence before you even speak to someone? If you do a good job for your client, they'll recommend you to other decision makers within the company. A recommendation already creates a degree of trust and confidence.

Get testimonials and recommendations from your existing clients and candidates, because it'll help to build confidence in new clients and candidates. Also ask for recommendations on LinkedIn. Testimonials create social proof and they're no different from product reviews you find on e-commerce websites. This reminds me. Please, write me a nice review and recommendation from where you bought my book, thank you.

Testimonials must come from clients and candidates and not from colleagues. If you're starting out in recruitment and you've not made your first placement, don't worry about this yet, it'll come.

MATCH THE CLIENT'S PERSONALITY

To build a relationship there must be mutual respect. Sometimes, recruitment consultants can give clients too much respect, and consequently get walked over. When I say match the client's personality I don't mean change yours, I mean adapt your behaviour to theirs. For example, some clients will challenge you, because their personality is one that likes to associate with strong dominating people. You might find this is common in certain industries. With such clients you'll earn their respect by challenging them back and, when relevant, disagreeing with them. You're the expert, so demonstrate your knowledge and expertise. However, avoid arguing or being confrontational with a client. That's not the same as being challenging.

Without sounding contradictory, it's important to be yourself. You can match the client's personality and still be yourself at the same time. Another common misconception is that to succeed in recruitment you need to be an extrovert. You can be an introvert and still be a great recruitment consultant.

REPUTATION SPREADS

I've often heard from candidates about terrible experiences with recruitment consultants. Candidates are especially good at spreading your reputation, both positively and negatively. If you treat your candidates right they'll recommend you to their friends, family and colleagues. They'll sing your praises during placements. Treat them poorly and you'll feel their repercussions. You never know who the candidate is related to, and they could become a hiring manager one day.

SHOW EMPATHY

Show empathy towards your clients and candidates. Empathy is an ability to recognise other people's emotions and being able to see the world through their eyes. For example, your client may be hesitant to use recruitment agencies, because they've had a bad experience. Your candidate may be too scared to hand in their notice to leave for the new job you've placed them in. You'll need to be able to recognise these emotions, because it will enable you to communicate with your clients and candidates on a deeper level.

SLOW IS SMOOTH AND SMOOTH IS FAST

The American military have a saying: "Slow is smooth and smooth is fast". Basically if you rush something you'll make mistakes which can mean restarting the task, but if you take your time to do things properly you'll get there faster.

I mentioned in an earlier section that you shouldn't be over familiar with clients. Rapport takes time to build, so don't try and rush it with personal questions and sleazy compliments. As you call your clients in a professional way your relationships will grow organically.

To conclude this section, let's recap what you need to do in order to develop relationships with your clients and candidates:

- Build trust
- Stay professional
- Be positive
- Instil confidence
- Adapt to their personality
- Take your time
- Do a good job
- Treat people correctly
- Show empathy

Meetings

A friend of mine, a successful recruitment consultant, once told me that: "It's very difficult to sell over the telephone. Instead sell the meeting, so you can sell in person".

That was good advice, but not 100 percent true. In larger complex sales a meeting may be a logical step in the relationship building process. However, in other sales environments clients may buy without ever having met the sales professional. This is especially true if they're buying in distress which means they need the product immediately. Therefore, you can indeed sell successfully over the telephone without ever meeting your client. However, this depends on your client, as some prefer not to have a meeting. Other clients might not work with you unless they've met you.

Some recruitment managers will feel, strongly, that

a meeting is an essential part of the recruitment process. This might be because this was how they were managed and targeted, or because a meeting is an essential part of your recruitment process in your industry. Always measure your sales-to-meeting ratio. I know a recruitment consultant who analysed his sales-to-meetings ratio and found that every sale he made was from clients he never met. Every client he had met had never given him a sale. He had been on about 20 meetings which, on average, took two hours including travel. That totalled up to 40 hours, which is equivalent to a week of selling over the telephone. Now, this could be because he didn't present himself strongly in meetings, or for some other reason. Regardless, it's an important ratio to be aware of.

Now I may appear to be against meetings. I'm not, I'm against being counter-productive. There are some clients who feel a meeting is essential before they work with you. For the rest of this section we'll concentrate on these clients.

A meeting with a client can help you progress the relationship forward. It's an opportunity for you to learn more about the client and for the client to learn more about you. You'll better understand their personality and how they act. At the same time, you'll get a feel for the culture and environment of the company. This should help you recruit the right candidates for them.

In this section I'll show you how to book meetings with clients and how to structure a sales meeting with your client.

GETTING MEETINGS

I'm going to let you into the biggest secret for getting your clients to meet with you. The secret is to ask. It really is that simple.

In the 'Learn to Ask' section of this book, I mentioned that when I first began in recruitment my manager challenged me as to why I wasn't getting any meetings with clients. It turned out the reason was because I wasn't asking my clients to meet with me. Once I started asking, by the end of my first year I had met with 90% of the clients on my patch.

Just ask if you can visit your client and wait for their response. At the end of your telephone call, if you've established your client's needs, reconfirm their needs and sell the benefits of your services. Then close the call with the following script:

You: (after you've reconfirmed their needs and your benefits) "The next logical step would be for us to meet. Do you have a spare 15 minutes that I could come out and see you?"

Once you've asked, stop talking and wait for their response.

Client: "Okay."

You: "Great. I have my diary open, when would be best for you?"

Client: "Friday at 2pm."

You: "That sounds good to me. Do you have an email address and I'll email you a calendar reminder.

Client: "Yes, it's..."

You: "Thank you, I look forward to seeing you then."

Keep it as basic as that and you can't go far wrong. Of course you'll come up against many objections, but instead of dwelling on the rejection acknowledge it and then move past it. For example:

You: "No problem, hopefully I'll get to meet you at some stage in the future."

If you've already spoken to your client previously

and have built up some connection, then try the following approach:

You: "Hi <client's name>. It's <your name> from <your company>.How are you?

Client: "Hi. I'm good thanks. How can I help you?"

You: "We've spoken a couple of times on the telephone and I'd like to be more than just a voice. Do you have a spare 15 minutes that I could come out and see you?"

If your client says "yes" then get a date in the diary. If they say "no", acknowledge it and then move past it. Ask more questions to build rapport and gather intelligence. For example:

You: "No problem, hopefully I'll get to meet you at some stage in the future. While I've got you on the telephone, do you want me to keep an eye out for any candidates for you?"

Or

You: "No problem, hopefully I'll get to meet you at some stage in the future. While I've got you on the telephone, I just want to run a candidate past you."

This way if the client is planning to recruit they will say "yes" and you can get a job description from them, or arrange to call them back.

Alternatively you can try and handle the objection and persuade the client that a meeting would be beneficial to them, which we will go through later in this section.

BLOCK BOOKING

Try to block book your meetings in specific areas. This will save you time, time that you'll want to use for selling. Block booking your meetings is when you visit several clients in one day who are all located in close proximity. That means they can be in the same company or in neighbouring companies. Some clients don't want to meet recruitment consultants when they're not recruiting. They feel that it's a waste of their time and your time. However, they'll be more inclined to meet you if they know you're in the area or in the same building. Try the following script.

You: "Hi <client's name>. It's <your name> from <company>."

Client: "Hi."

You: "On <date> I'm visiting <company> which is

just down the road from you. I should be finished about <time>. Since I'm in the area would you be free for a quick meeting?"

Rich recruiters use this technique even if they don't have any meetings booked with neighbouring clients. They'll call a client to say they're visiting with a neighbouring company, and use this to meet with their prospect.

Notice I said "visit" and not "meeting". Now I want to state and remind you that you should always use ethics when selling and never push bad candidates on to your clients, or force candidates into jobs they don't want. As well as it being wrong, it'll also come back and cause you problems in the future. Never lie to your clients to get them to buy.

However, while you shouldn't lie, you'll at times need to bend the rules of the game. You won't get far in recruitment, business, or life by following all of the rules. Sometimes you need to bend them. You don't need a meeting to be able to "visit" a company. Just visit their reception on the same day and pass over your company brochure to the receptionist. Then politely ask the receptionist to pass it to your client. Technically you've visited the company and no lies have been told. You can then use the brochure as an excuse to call the client the next day and ask if they received it okay. If the client your meeting asks you how your visit went with the other company, tell them it went well.

SALARY SURVEY

Another way to get your clients to meet you is through a salary survey. A salary survey is an informative booklet about the average salaries in the industry you recruit for. The survey usually shows information on salaries in different geographical areas, what candidates are looking for, what makes employees happy in their role, and any other relevant information.

Some clients like salary surveys, because they like to know if they're currently being paid the market rate. They'll also want to know if they're paying their employees the right amount, so they don't lose key staff to other organisations. You can use the salary survey to get a meeting with your client, for example:

You: "We've produced our new salary survey. It shows the current average salaries in your industry, what employees want and what candidates are looking for. Are you free for me to come and visit you to talk you through it?"

If your recruitment company currently doesn't produce salary surveys you can approach a market research company to do the survey for you. Then have them produce it into booklets to provide to your clients.

OBJECTION HANDLING FOR GETTING MEETINGS

When you try to book meetings with your clients some will give you objections. In some cases clients give you objections just to see how you handle them. In this section I'll go over some common objections clients give to avoid a meeting, and what you can say to handle the objection.

Client: "I'm not recruiting at the moment."

As mentioned earlier, some clients don't see the point in seeing recruitment consultants unless they're currently recruiting. In this case try the following script:

You: "Hi <client's name>. It's <your name> from <your company>. How are you?"

Client: "Hi, I'm good thanks. How can I help you?"

You: "We've spoken a couple of times on the telephone and I'd like to be more than just a voice. Do you have a spare 15 minutes that I could come out and see you?"

Client: "I don't think that's necessary at the moment. We're not recruiting."

You: "I was hoping you would say that. It's actually best we meet when you're not recruiting. It will save you time in the long run. I'll know exactly the type of candidate you look for, for when you do recruit."

Another line you can use:

You: "I'm interested in your company and while there's nothing happening now, I genuinely want to know you and understand your business for when you do recruit."

Another common objection from clients is:

Client: "I'm too busy."

Some possible ways to handle this objection:

You: "I'll only take up 10 minutes of your time."

You: "I'll just pop in briefly."

You: "I know you are that's why a meeting now is

best. It will save you having lots of agencies sending you lots of irrelevant CV's and bombarding you will telephone calls."

You: "Why don't we book a meeting far ahead when you have more time, let's say in a couple of months? It really will be brief. I have my diary open, do you have a less busy time available?"

You: "It'll mean I can get the candidate right first time, so it will actually save you time."

PREPARING FOR THE MEETING

"By failing to prepare, you are preparing to fail."-
Benjamin Franklin

The first thing you should do is check whether you have the correct address of where your meeting is. Some companies have multiple sites, which can be confusing. Always clarify this on the telephone when you book the meeting. However, if you haven't, and you're hesitant to call back, you can call the receptionist and they will clarify this with you.

Next you should find a colleague who can go to the sales meeting with you. A sales meeting is always better with two people for several reasons:

- Your colleague can take notes while you communicate with the client
- The meeting is less intimidating for you if there are two of you
- You can review the meeting afterwards to ensure nothing was missed

Plan your route to the client beforehand, so you're not late. If you expect you're going to be late call the client and let them know. While you should do everything in your power to be on time sometimes unexpected events happen. Clients usually don't mind if you're late as long as you have the manners to inform them in advance. If you don't inform them they'll spend that time waiting for you reflecting on how poor your service must be.

Now you know exactly how you're going to get to your client you'll want to know more about your client and their company. You should:

- Speak to your colleagues who are dealing, or have dealt with the company and ask them for any information you should know. Clients dislike having to repeat basic information about the company to different consultants.
- Check the company's website so that you fully understand their services and products.
- Type the name of the company into a search

engine, such as Google to see if there is anything in the news. Sometimes your visit can fall around the time of a merger, acquisition, growth or even around the time of job threats.

• Do a search on your client on Google and LinkedIn to identify any information about their professional background or interests. You can use this information to ask them more personal rapport-building questions.

If you find out any interesting information about the company, or you're unsure about anything, bring it up in the meeting. There have been times when I've had to ask exactly what the company does as it wasn't explicit on their website. The client will usually agree it's confusing.

As a recruitment consultant you'll know how important first impressions are. As soon as the client sees you they'll start to make a visual judgement about whether you have the ability to recruit for them. How you dress can depend on what industry you recruit for and the dress code of your company. I know a recruitment company that doesn't like their recruitment consultants to wear a suit, as it could intimidate their clients. In this particular case this company deals with primary school staff.

The rule is always to dress better than you think

you should, or one level above. The reason that dressing smartly is important is that your clients subconsciously perceive a well-dressed recruitment consultant as a higher quality product. They will subconsciously feel that if you can take care of yourself you can also take care of them. Imagine if you were going for surgery and in your consultation the surgeon turned up looking scruffy. You'd probably question whether they cared and whether you were in safe hands.

Dressing smart is only halfway there. Ensure your hair is neatly cut and that you have brushed your teeth. If you haven't had time to brush your teeth and have had to resort to chewing gum. Lose the chewing gum before you meet the client. There is nothing more unattractive than chewing gum in front of your client.

There are several things you should take with you to every sales meeting:

- Several business cards
- Several working pens
- A clean A4 writing pad
- Carefully selected CV's of good, relevant candidates
- Job specification forms
- Your company's sales literature

• Terms of business

People like to touch and feel things before they buy. It's why clothes shops have changing rooms and why you're encouraged to take cars on a test drive. Once you've tried the product you're more likely to make a purchase. As recruitment consultants you're selling a service, so it can be more difficult for your clients to get a feel for your product. By taking business cards, company literature and some relevant CV's you make it more tangible for your client. They can now touch and feel your services.

SALES MEETING STRUCTURE

The best recruitment consultants don't sell, instead they consult their clients. The following sales meeting structure will help your meetings feel more consultative rather than like a sales pitch:

- **Introduction** – making the client feel at ease
- **Questioning and consultation** – learning about the client and their problems
- **Reconfirming** – demonstrating you've listened
- **Selling** – showing them how you can solve their problems
- **Closing the meeting** – asking for their business

Introduction

The introduction is when you first meet the client and you start to make them feel at ease. You might meet the client in the reception area and then walk with them to their office. It's important to remember that from this point the introduction has already started. In other cases you might be taken to their office by an assistant. In this case your introduction with the client starts when you're introduced to them by the assistant. However, your client may ask the assistant what they thought of you, so treat the assistant how you would treat your client.

Always greet the client with a firm handshake and a smile. Earlier in the book we discussed how clients like you to stick to business. However, it can be awkward to go straight into business if you've met your client in the reception area and you need to travel together to their office. You can make the conversation both personal and business-related at the same time. For example,

You: "I noticed on your LinkedIn profile you used to work in America. That must have been fun. How did that come about?"

This has an impact on several different levels: firstly, it shows you've prepared for the meeting; secondly, most people love to talk about themselves; thirdly, while it's personal it's still business-related, so the client won't feel threatened.

Another example:

You: "Thank you for meeting with me today. You must be so busy with the recent expansion."

Don't fall into the trap of looking around the room for an interesting topic to discuss, such as a photograph or a golf trophy. They'll have met many sales professionals who've wasted their time talking about non business-related subjects. By keeping your introductions business-related, but on a personal level, you can guide them into the next stage of the meeting with ease, which is questioning and consulting.

Questioning and consultation

At this stage you'll ask the client questions about their business, their department and about recruitment. Your client should be doing most of the talking while you do most of the listening. Ask them lots of open questions to get them to open up, but ask closed questions to get specific answers. Save the closed questions for the later part of the meeting. Reread the section on questioning and SPIN® selling at the beginning of the book to refresh your memory.

The information you should be looking for includes:

- Department / company structure – ask for a structure chart
- Department size
- Turnover
- Product / service range
- Locations
- Computer systems
- How they normally recruit
- The benefits of working for the company
- What problems they've had / do they have
- Whether they have a preferred supplier list
- Which other agencies they use and why
- What they like and dislike about recruitment companies
- What a good candidate looks like to them
- What problems they face regarding recruitment
- What effects these problems have on the wider business
- If there's anyone else you should be talking to

If the client has already given you specific information on the telephone, don't ask the same questions again. However, you should reconfirm what they've told you over the telephone by reflecting it back to them and asking them if the information you have is correct. This will demonstrate that you've been listening to them.

We perceive people who cannot hold eye contact as untrustworthy and unconfident, so maintain eye contact with your client in between writing notes. It's better to get your colleague to write the bulk of the notes while you stay fully engaged in the conversation.

Reconfirming

This stage involves reconfirming what the client has said to you. It shows the client you've listened and understood what they've said. It also enables you to correct anything.

To guide the client into this stage you might say something like the following.

You: "Okay, so you dislike it when recruitment companies send you hundreds of CV's. This is making your job harder..."

At this point the client will be nodding and agreeing with you, which puts you in an ideal position for actually selling.

Selling

This is the only stage when you actually sell. While

you'll have your standard pitch you'll want to tailor part of it to match what the client has told you during the questioning and consultation stage.

Ensure you sell the benefits of your recruitment services, for example:

You: "Your current method of recruitment means you're getting too many CV's. As a result of this you're being pulled away from your core duties. I'll only ever send you 2 to 3 relevant CV's, which will save you the hassle of going through hundreds of irrelevant CV's. We vet and reference all candidates, so you won't need to do this if you hire our candidate, again saving you more time..."

Once you've pitched your services to the client, you'll want to close the meeting. Before you do this make sure there are no barriers or reservations by asking the client if there are any barriers to taking the next logical step.

Closing the meeting

There are three situations the meeting will be taking place under: one, the client is recruiting; two, the client isn't recruiting; three, you're already helping them recruit.

Here are some example closes for each situation:

The client isn't currently recruiting:

- "How would you feel about me working on your next vacancy?"

The client is recruiting:

- "The next logical step is to take a job specification."
- "The next logical steps would be to send you CV's. I can send you a CV by Friday."

You're already helping them recruit:

- "Out of the CV's I've sent you, which do you like and which don't you like?"
- "Would you like to interview any of these candidates?"
- "When can you run interviews?"

Remember, closing is simply asking your client for their business or some progression and then keeping quiet until your client speaks first.

SALES MEETING BODY LANGUAGE

Body language is very important in sales. You need to be aware of your body language as well as the client's. The subject is in-depth and there are entire books about body language. While I think being able to read body language is vital to being good at sales, it can be over analysed. To prevent over analysis I'll just touch on the subject.

Your Body Language

This is body language you should adopt for your sales meetings.

Acknowledging body language – Recruitment consulting and sales is all about listening. To demonstrate you're listening nod your head and say things such as: "yes", "okay", "I see", "really", "uh-huh".

Mirroring – If you observe couples and friends you'll notice their body language is similar to one another. They subconsciously mirror each other's body language and gestures. When people mirror each other's body language they're saying "we're the same". You can create this feeling by mirroring the body language of your client. I recommend you do this a quarter to half-way into the meeting and don't do it too much, as it needs to be subtle. Judge what you should mirror, as I've been in meetings where the client has sat back with their arms behind their head. This probably wouldn't have been good to mirror.

Confident body language – Confident body language is when we open up our bodies and expose ourselves. No, not your private parts, although that would take a great deal of confidence to do in a client meeting, let's leave that one off the list. In simplistic terms if a tortoise is confident that no predators are around it will have all its vulnerable body parts exposed. However, if it feels in danger it will hide in its shell. Translating this into humans, you should keep your body language open by keeping your head up, shoulders back, arms uncrossed and legs uncrossed.

The following is body language you should avoid in your sales meeting:

Low confidence – As I stated earlier, when animals feel in danger their confidence levels drop and they retreat into themselves like the tortoise. This is to protect vulnerable body parts, make themselves smaller to be less of a target and to hide from their predators. Humans also display this type of body language when they lack confidence. They turtle their head into their shoulders, hide behind their hands when they talk, cross their arms and cross their legs. Avoid all these types of body language and try to open out more. The very act of opening your body language will make you feel confident, because your emotions follow what your body does.

No eye contact – I mentioned earlier that people who cannot hold eye contact are perceived as untrustworthy. It also shows a lack of confidence. Keep looking your client in the eye. It's fine and natural to break eye contact and you should, because too much eye contact is threatening. So what's the right balance? Keep looking your client in the eye, but break eye contact to write notes and during conversations.

Their Body Language – Throughout the meeting you'll want to assess their body language, so that you can read their mood and adapt your questioning.

Barriers – When we don't like something we try to put a barrier between us and what we don't like. A classic example is hiding behind a pillow when watching a horror film. When people don't like someone or what someone says they'll cross their arms and lean away. During your meeting if you see this display of behaviour you'll need to overcome the objection before moving forward. Try a different tactic to get them to open up. However, be aware of your environment, if the room is cold your client is likely to cross their arms and legs to keep warm rather than because you said something.

Clock watching and fidgeting – If your client keeps fidgeting, looking at their watch or the clock on the wall, they're likely saying I've got somewhere else to be. Never assume, so to ensure it's not a passing glance or an uncomfortable chair ask them how they're doing for time, if they need to go they'll tell you. It's not good to rush your pitch and leave. It can sound desperate, the same as when you rush what you need to say on the telephone. The client won't be listening properly either. Instead, explain how important this meeting is to you and how much you'd value working with them, so ask them if you can rearrange for a later date.

Buying signs – The client is buying into you when they display gravity defying body language. This will look like steepled hands, raised eye brows, sitting forward, nodding of the head, smiling and verbally agreeing with you.

Closing body language – When you close a client and ask for their business using any of the closing techniques we discussed earlier, the client is likely to squirm in their seat and shift around. This isn't necessarily a bad thing. Stay relaxed and stay silent. Let them speak first.

NEGOTIATING

Negotiating for me is always the most fun part of recruitment. The key is to make everyone feel like they've won. When you and your client both win you help to build a stronger relationship. Always think long term, and never think short term. If you begin negotiating and you win, but the client feels they've lost, then they're unlikely to ever to do business with you again. If you negotiate and you lose while the client wins you'll be feeling as if your skills aren't valued, and you won't make money.

My first rule for negotiating is: try to avoid negotiating. Even though I think it's the most fun part of recruitment and business in general, it's best if the client accepts your terms of business. I've seen recruitment consultants, especially new ones, say to their client: "Our fee is 20% of the salary, but our fees are negotiable." Avoid making statements like this, because you're inviting your client to negotiate.

My second rule for negotiating is: always start high. You can always lower your fee, but you can never go higher once you have given the client a number. There is also a psychological effect of going in high, because it makes any lower number feel like a win to your client.

A psychological experiment was carried out where two researchers asked random people for money. Let's call them researcher one and researcher two. Both researchers asked the random people for £1 coins, but researcher two collected more £1 coins than researcher one. The reason for this was that researcher two at first asked for £20. People were quite rightly shocked and turned researcher two down. However, on being rejected researcher two immediately asked the same person for £1 instead. Strangers saw £1 as a far lesser amount and handed over a £1 coin.

Recently a very well-known charity tried the above technique on me. A sales professional called and asked me to increase my monthly donation by a larger amount. Not wanting to increase my monthly donation without thought, I said I'd have to review it. The sales professional changed tactic and asked if I'd like to increase my donations by a substantially lower amount. I instantly agreed. Once I put the phone down I realised how he achieved this sale and I couldn't help but smile at his sales ability. Do note that in this case the sales professional can get away with asking for a 'substantially lower amount', because I'm already paying them money. Therefore, any additional money is a bonus. Never lower your fee to an amount that'll cause you to lose money.

Your recruitment company will no doubt have terms of business. The terms of business will contain the fee rates of your services, which will probably be already high, or at least competitive. This makes life easier for you, as you can use it to go in at that level. When you're recruiting over the telephone the client will typically ask you what your fee rate is. They may ask you as a general enquiry even when they're not recruiting. Some clients will ask you what your fee rate is before allowing you to take a job specification. Others will discuss fees with you during the job specification. Have your fee rates cut out and stuck where they can be easily seen, so you can read them off.

If the client is inexperienced or has been flippant, what usually happens is the client will not even look at your fee rates in your terms of business until they're ready to buy your candidate. They'll go through the entire requirement process including interviews then decide they want the candidate. Then they'll read the fee rate in your terms of business. In this case you're in a stronger position to negotiate. If you've done a huge amount of work, and the client has had you working extremely hard, don't feel bad for telling the client that you can't lower the fee rate. Tell them how hard you've worked. If your recruitment has been relatively easy and the client tries to negotiate a price create a win-win situation by providing a fair price.

My third rule for negotiating is: never speak first. The first to speak is the first to lose. If you feel that negotiating is the only option, when a client asks you to lower the fee rate, never give them a number first. Remember, once you give them a number you can never go back up. Instead, bounce it back to them and ask them what they had in mind. When you ask the client to give you a number, you'll hear in their voice that you've put them on the back foot. The reason they're on the back foot is because they fear that their offer will be rejected. They'll typically say something like: "I was thinking about x%". You can now take this offer if it's a good offer, or reject it by asking for a higher fee rate. You may even say something such as: "I'm sorry, but I couldn't possibly work at that rate, due to the amount of work involved. I could do z%."

My fourth rule for negotiating is: don't care about the deal. This sounds like a weird rule, but hear me out. Have you ever noticed that when you're in a relationship you get more offers from other people? Do you notice when you're in a job you get approached by people for other jobs? Do you notice when you have jobs to fill you then get more jobs much more easily when you do sales calls?

This happens for two main reasons. The first is the law of being relaxed. When you have lots of jobs on your board to fill, your sales calls have a relaxed, carefree tone. This is because you don't need the business. When you have a partner, you're more relaxed around other people and you're not trying to impress. This makes you more attractive to other people. The next time you're in a bar or club observe people in the room. You'll be able to tell who's single and who's not.

The second reason is due to the law of scarcity. People want more of the things there are less of. In 2003, British airways announced they'd no longer be operating the twice daily Concorde flight from London to New York, as it had become uneconomical to run. The very next day sales increased. Nothing had changed about the service of the flight it had simply become a scarce resource, so people wanted it more. You'll also find you suffer from this with candidates. The candidate that doesn't want to apply for your role will be the most attractive one.

Negotiating has the same psychology. If you're dealing with only one client and you're desperate for a deal, the client will sense this and go in for the kill, because they subconsciously sense your vulnerability. However, if you have lots of business going on and the client offers you a ridiculously lower fee, you're more likely say "Thank you, but no thank you." Your relaxed and confident attitude will no doubt put them off trying to negotiate in the first place, or negotiating too hard.

Therefore, always play with a poker face and never show your cards. Even if this is the only deal you have on the table, act as if you're in demand and your time is scarce.

My fifth rule for negotiating is: never give anything without something in return. If your client asks you to lower your fee rate, and says they absolutely cannot go any higher, you should ask for exclusivity, or to be their preferred supplier for future jobs. Try to see that everything has a value during your negotiation. If they take something away, you ask them to replace it with something of equal value. You might say something, such as: "If you can agree to give me exclusivity, I'll agree to drop the rate to 15%."

My sixth rule for negotiating is: hide your emotions. Professional buyers will try to reduce the fee as low as possible. Don't take this personally, it's just a game and not an attack on your skills. Nothing bad can come from negotiating, even if the deal doesn't go through there are plenty more out there. Therefore, you have nothing to be nervous or worried about. The best way not to sound nervous is to keep your sentences short and direct, for example:

Client: "I can only work with you at 15%".

Nerves Consultant: "Erm... let me check with my Director and I'll get back to you", or "Erm... I'm not sure, can we not work at 18%?"

Confident Consultant: "I can only work at 20%."

If you wanted to sound more empathetic:

"I wish I could, but I cannot go lower than 20%."

Confident Consultant: "I can go down to 19%, if you agree to leave this vacancy with me for at least two weeks?"

Confident Consultant: "I couldn't respect myself if I dropped my fees to 15%."

My seventh rule for negotiating is: walk away if the deal is unprofitable. If the client is squeezing your profit or demanding unrealistic expectations then you should walk away and find a more profitable client.

In summary my seven rules for negotiation are:

- Try to avoid negotiating
- Always start high
- Never speak first
- Don't care about the deal
- Never give anything without something in return
- Hide your emotions
- Walk away if the deal is unprofitable

WRITTEN SALES

If you want to be a rich recruitment consultant, not only do you have to be good in verbal sales, but also in your writing. Your ability to sell through the written form will dramatically increase your sales. Everything you write is a sell, every email, every e-shot and every blog.

In this section I'll show you how to improve your sales writing skills. There is a more detailed section specifically on e-shots later in the book. In this section we'll concentrate on emails, but the principles can be taken and adapted to other sales literature such as brochures.

Firstly, I want to draw a distinction between marketing and selling with closing. You're always marketing and selling, but this doesn't always lead to a close. When you email a client something as simple as:

Hi Steven,

Thank you for your time on the telephone earlier. I've attached a news article that I thought you'd be interested in with regards to our conversation.

Kind regards,

Andrew Leong

You're marketing, selling and consulting, but you're not trying to close a deal. This is a simple way to connect with and build a relationship with your client. It shows them you're interested in them, and that you're more than just a person who's trying to take their money. You don't need to close a deal on every occasion for you to be good at sales.

USE AIDA

AIDA is a well-known acronym used in marketing and advertising to help with copywriting. It describes a common list of events that may occur when your client engages with your sales literature. You should check that your sales literature contains the following elements:

A = Attention: attract the attention of the customer.

I = Interest: raise your customer's interest by writing about information that is relevant to them, potentially solves their problems and offers them advantages and benefits.

D = Desire: using specific words and language patterns will create desire.

A = Action: make it extremely obvious what the client has to do next if they want to progress forward, and make it as simple as possible.

GET TO THE POINT

There is common misconception that if you provide lots of information with facts and figures the client will be so impressed that they just *have* to buy. Instead, what happens is the client will see a massive email that they won't bother reading and it'll be deleted. If by some chance they do read it, by the time they get to the bottom of the email they'll have lost the point.

For that reason, you need to get to the point in as few words as possible. Steve Jobs, the late CEO of Apple, was a master at this. When I was younger I used a device called a Walkman to listen to music while on the go. It was bulky and ugly. I had to carry with me several tapes that stored the music. Each tape could only hold about 12 songs, so it was very inconvenient. Then Steve Jobs created the "iPod", a highly sophisticated device for storing and listening to music. It did away with tapes and CDs and it looked good.

On selling the iPod, Steve Jobs did it beautifully with the following phrase:

"1,000 songs in your pocket."

No technical jargon, just straight to the point. Keep this in mind when you write your emails and e-shots. Get to the point in as few words as possible. Clients are more likely to read your emails if they're short and they can see the whole message on their screen without having to scroll down.

EMAIL STRUCTURE

Different emails have different structures and as you build rapport with your client your emails may become less formal, but no less professional. In other words, you'll write more conversationally.

However, to begin with it's always best practice to write your emails in a structured way. If we return back to the power of three your emails should be structured as follows:

1. Strong introduction or opening

2.   Main body
3.   Close / call to action

Following this structure while keeping your emails short will make them look professional. This will attract the recipient and persuade them to read.

GOOD ENGLISH

You don't need to have a degree in English to be good at writing sales literature. You can massively improve your English language with just a few simple tips. The famous writer and author George Orwell states six rules for effective writing:

1.   Never use a metaphor, simile, or other figure of speech which you are used to seeing in print

2.   Never use a long word where a short one will do

3.   If it is possible to cut a word out, always cut it out

4.   Never use the passive where you can use the active

5.   Never use a foreign phrase, a scientific word, or a jargon word if you can think of an everyday English equivalent

6.   Break any of these rules sooner than say anything outright barbarous

WAYS TO IMPROVE YOUR WRITTEN SALES

One of the best ways to improve your writing is to copy others until you find your own style. You'll only want to copy those who are successful, so ask your manager for a copy of all the e-shots and emails that have ever generated an enquiry, especially if the enquiry has come from a new client.

Look at each email and e-shot to see if they have any trends. Look at the use of language, the structure, the length and the use of formatting. Look to see if the e-shots used any numbers and percentages. Then see how many times numbers were used. Were they used lots or were they used sparingly?

You should notice some common features, but also some unique features that you can start adopting in your writing.

If your recruitment company hasn't kept any winning e-shots or emails, ask your manager to implement this going forward. Whenever you hear of a colleague pulling in a client from an e-shot or an email ask them if you can have a copy.

The next time you buy something save the description or the sell, even if it's just a customer review that convinced you to buy. Then analyse the writing and see if it could be implemented in your sales writing.

EXAMPLE EMAILS

I always learn best when I see an example. In this section I'll write some basic examples that you can use to adapt into you own style. I've specifically chosen these emails, because they got a reply from clients.

Introduction email after your first telephone call:

Hi <name>,

Thank you for your time on the telephone earlier.

As discussed, I'm a specialist <industry> recruitment consultant working for a company called <agency name>.

<agency name> has been around for X number of years and we offer a tailored and professional recruitment service to our clients.

I have attached a brochure for your information, but you can also find out more by visiting <agency website>.

I will call you towards the end of the week to col-

lect your thoughts, but if I can help you beforehand, please, do not hesitate to contact me via telephone on: <number> or via email <email address>

Kind regards

<your name>

When you cannot get the client on the telephone

Hi <name>,

We've not spoken before my name is <your name> and I work for a company called <your company>. I've not been able to catch you on the telephone.

I'm a specialist recruitment consultant for <industry> in <sector> based in your local area.

I'm keen to work with you and wondered what the best way is to communicate with you?

Kind regards,

<your name>

Email after a Promotional Campaign

I once sent out a promotional brochure with a chocolate bar called a Kit Kat. I then sent this email to the clients I couldn't get on the telephone:

Subject: *How was your Kit Kat?*

Hi <name>,

We've not spoken before my name is <your name> and I work for a company called <your company>. I've not been able to catch you on the telephone yet to introduce myself more formally.

I sent you a package recently and I hope you enjoyed the contents. As you know, I'm a specialist recruitment consultant for <industry> in <sector> based in your local area.

I would relish the opportunity to work with you. What would be the best way to communicate with you?

Kind regards,

<your name>

SALES WORDS

There are certain words that you can use to make your e-shots, job adverts and emails more persuasive. Type into an internet search engine: "sales

words" and you'll get several websites offering you
a comprehensive list of words that you can refer to.
Here are a few sales words that you can use:

- Accomplish
- Achieve
- Award-winning
- Benefit
- Best
- Clear-cut
- Competitive
- Complimentary
- Dependable
- Effective
- Experienced
- Ensure
- Excited
- First-class
- Free
- Guarantee
- Improve
- New
- Now
- Proven
- Quality
- Qualified
- Results
- Safe
- Simple

- Top
- Unique
- Winner
- You
- Your

Use these words intelligently and don't fall into the habit of using the same words otherwise your messages will lose their effect. In the recruitment industry you'll find that consultants use the same repetitive phrases, such as:

- Hit the ground running
- Dynamic role
- Forward thinking
- Put a face to the name
- Touch base
- This role / candidate is perfect for you

It's fine to use these words, but to differentiate yourself from your competitors, who will be using these stock phrases, think creatively. There are online thesauruses that you can use to search for alternative words. If you prefer a physical thesaurus buy one and keep it on your desk.

When writing an email to a client watch out for how many times you use the words "I", "I'm" and "I've" versus "you" and "your". If you use the word "I" too much the email becomes about you. The email should always be about your client. You'll want to make the reader feel special, as if you're talking to them personally. To achieve this use the words "you" and "your" more than "I".

PROOFREADING

You have a busy and demanding job. You're running round making telephone calls, visiting clients, interviewing candidates and chasing targets. No matter how confident you are as a sales writer you'll on occasion feel rushed and short of time. While established clients do turn a blind eye to the occasional spelling mistake or typo, an email to a new client must be perfect. This is because it's their first impression of you.

When you're exhausted and you feel that you've no time to spare, you'll still have to write e-shots, emails, job adverts and blogs. This can lead to you rushing your written sales work. Do stop and slow down, because once you click the send button you can't get it back. Always get a colleague to check your work and if necessary save your work and come back to it with a fresh pair of eyes.

OUTSOURCING YOUR SALES LITERATURE

Outsourcing is when you pay someone else to do a job for you. Technically, recruitment consulting is outsourcing, as companies outsource their recruitment to you. Virtually everything can be outsourced and I'm a massive fan of it.

If you want to you can outsource the creation of your sales literature for very little cost.

I doubt the recruitment company you work for will pay for your outsourcing work. After all, that work is what they're paying you to do. However, that doesn't mean you can't pay for it yourself. You can find freelance writers who will write sales literature from as little as £6 upwards. Checkout the website 'PeoplePerHour' and you'll find people who can write your emails, sales literature, blogs and anything else you need.

Why would you pay for someone else to write sales literature for you? If you're not a natural writer it can sometimes take several hours to write a good piece of work. You might just be extremely busy and not have the time to write something with passion. Therefore, for £6+ it would be worth someone else doing it, so you can either spend more time on the telephone or more time on your social life.

BE LUCKY

Some people are just luckier than others. Some people are born into a wealthy family. Some people are born with an amazing talent. Some people are born with society's perception of good luck. However, some people are born unlucky.

While you cannot change where you were born, or to a degree, your physical appearance, you can influence your luck.

"The harder I work the luckier I get" – Gary Player

Gary Player is a South African professional golfer, widely regarded as one of the greatest players in the history of golf. Over his career, he won nine major championships on the regular tour and six Champions Tour major championship victories, as well as three Senior British Open Championships on the European Senior Tour. After he won the U.S. Open the commentator said: "Gary, unbelievable, you got so lucky." Gary replied: "The harder I work, the luckier I get."

I'm fascinated by luck, and I noticed successful recruitment consultants just seemed luckier than the not-so-successful ones. It had nothing to do with their looks, or where they were born or who they were born to. Recruitment and sales over the telephone strips all that away. Nevertheless, they were extremely lucky. I couldn't believe or accept that they were born with this magical power called luck.

I wanted to find out why some people are luckier than others, so I set off to find out why. "Luckily", a man called Robert Wiseman did the research and experiments for me. He then produced a very interesting book called *The Luck Factor*. I recommend you buy and read his book, it's fascinating.

He conducted research and experiments on the lives of people who were lucky and unlucky. One simple experiment he conducted was to discover whether this was due to differences in their ability to spot such opportunities.

He gave both lucky and unlucky people a newspaper, and asked them to look through it and tell him how many photographs were inside.

Richard had secretly placed a large message half-way through the newspaper saying: *Stop counting you have won £100.* The message took up half of the page and was written in a size that was more than two inches high. While it was clear for everyone to see, the unlucky people missed it and the lucky people found it.

He concluded that unlucky people are generally more anxious than lucky people, and this anxiety prevents them from noticing opportunities. As a result, they miss opportunities because they're too focused on looking for something else. Unlucky people go to a party intent on finding their perfect partner and miss opportunities to make good friends with someone who isn't their perfect partner. They look through newspapers determined to find certain types of job adverts and miss other types of jobs.

That was just one experiment Richard did to identify one factor of luck, which is that lucky people have a relaxed attitude to life.

Luck is an important tool for becoming a rich recruiter, but thankfully you can increase your luck. In this section, I'll discuss Richard's four principles of luck and how you can apply them to recruitment.

Principle One: Maximise Chance Opportunities

Lucky people create, notice and act upon chance opportunities. They do this in three ways: networking, adopting a relaxed attitude to life, and being open to new experiences.

Talk to anybody and everyone. If you're standing in a queue in the supermarket, or sitting next to someone in a coffee shop, strike up a conversation. You have no idea what impact this person could have on your life, or you could have on theirs. They could be the decision maker, or the PA of a director of the company you're trying to do business with. In this case, not only have you just made a new friend, you've increased your chances of meeting your client. Earlier, we touched on the importance of having open body language in sales meetings. You should adopt having open body language in your everyday surroundings. You'll become more approachable to other people.

Learn to relax and take up a relaxed approach to life. This can be difficult in the recruitment industry, with targets, difficult candidates and it just being a very competitive environment. However, you must learn to be relaxed. Meditate if needed. Take time away from your desk and go for walk. If you're a manager, then do things to relax your team. Once you're relaxed, read the newspapers about your patch. You're more likely to spot stories about new companies being set up, or companies going through change. These are opportunities to make telephone calls and create business.

When you're outside of work, try new things. These can be such things as going to new restaurants, travelling different routes, and participating in new hobbies. These new experiences will bring you new opportunities.

One thing I was encouraged to do by my manager, if I was having a typically bad time on the telephones when clients weren't answering, was to call candidates instead. This not only meant I got to speak to people, but I picked up leads too.

Principle Two: Listening to Lucky Hunches

Lucky people make effective decisions by listening to their gut feelings and they take steps to actively boost their intuitive abilities.

In recruitment you're constantly dealing with people. You'll get gut feelings about candidates, whether they just seem unreliable, untrustworthy, or a letdown. You'll know this, through their behaviour. They'll be late to your interview. They won't return your calls for days. They'll have excuses for why they can't provide references. You'll just know they're not right. Similarly, you'll meet candidates who you think are amazing. If you have a bad gut feeling about a candidate, then don't work with them. It'll cause you more trouble down the road when they pull out of the interview with the client, or they don't even show up.

You'll even get gut feelings about clients. You'll sense they're trying to screw you and steal your candidate when they start asking you for the candidate's email address before an interview.

At times when you're desperate for a job you'll push those unreliable candidates onto clients and work with bad clients. You'll hope that it all works out, but it never does and you know it won't. Don't waste your time, destroy your reputation or give yourself the headache by doing this.

You'll get better at this the longer you're in recruitment. Wiseman recommends that you take up activities like meditation and walking to clear your mind of other thoughts. I know you'll be strapped for time, but time invested in yourself will give you a good return.

Principle Three: Expect Good Fortune
Lucky people are certain that the future is going to

be full of good fortune enabling them to fulfil their dreams and ambitions. Their expectations become self-fulfilling prophecies, which help lucky people persist in the face of failure, and to shape their interactions with others in a positive way.

I worked a desk next to a girl who's a good friend of mine. She would always get jobs every time she did sales calls. She would openly say, "I think I'm a lucky person". Little did she know that this positive affirmation was a self-fulfilling prophecy.

When you're going through a dry spell, or you're just starting out, it's important to remain positive about the future. Stay relaxed and keep making those calls. The more calls you make, the more emails and e-shots you send, the better you'll become at them. At the same time, more clients will remember your name and more opportunities will come about. Lucky people don't quit, they keep on trying and trying until they succeed. Even if it takes a year, even if it takes two years just to get your desk up and running, don't give up.

Imagine you have a company you're trying to work with, but you cannot get past the gatekeeper. If you keep calling, one day that gatekeeper will be off sick, or will have moved to a different job and you'll get through. One day you'll find a candidate who worked for the company and they'll give you a direct line for the decision maker to take their reference. These opportunities will only occur if you keep persevering, but you'll only keep persevering if you know these opportunities will happen. Now you know they will, *believe* they will.

Principle Four: Turn Bad Luck to Good Luck

Even lucky people face misfortune in life, but they don't see it as misfortune. Instead, they instinctively imagine how things could have been worse. They do not dwell on their misfortune, but take control of their situation.

The famous and brilliant business man Donald Trump once tried to buy a newspaper company. He negotiated the deal and told everyone how good it was. However, he unexpectedly caught the flu and he had to postpone the closing of the deal until he was better. This was unusual for Trump, because according to him he hardly ever gets sick. The seller called him and said they couldn't wait for him, so they were offering the newspaper company to someone else. He lost the deal. Sounds like bad luck. Several years later this flu turned out to be very good luck. The newspaper company is now worth far less than what Trump was going to pay for it. It would have lost him a fortune. Good luck can often be bizarrely disguised as misfortune. I recommend reading more about Donald Trump, he is a fantastic business man. This particular extract was taken from Trump and Zanker's book: *Think Big.*

Luck is also how a person perceives a situation and whether they see the good or the bad in it. If you fall down the stairs and break your arm, an unlucky person will dwell on the negatives and how life is against them. A lucky person will see the positives and believe they're lucky for not breaking their neck. Two similar situations, but two very different thought processes.

I was once recruiting for a very large well-known multinational company. In fact I ate one of their products for breakfast this morning while writing this book. After kicking and fighting, they finally let me recruit for them. I had the perfect candidate and I was sure it was a winning placement. My candidate went missing and then pulled out at the last minute for another job. I had to go back to my client with my tail between my legs and tell them my candidate pulled out of the interview. I was gutted, heartbroken and demoralised. A month later I received an email from the same company asking me to help them with another vacancy. Even though I hadn't placed the job, they were impressed by the CV's I had sent them and I was on their preferred suppliers list. Even good can come from misfortune.

As I was going over this chapter I came across a story in a newspaper that I want to share. The story is about a scrap metal dealer who bought a golden egg at a bric-a-brac market, because he thought he'd make money on it. He bought it for £8,000. After failing to sell it because people thought it was too expensive, he did a Google search to discover it was a £20 million Fabergé Egg. The newspaper states: *He had no luck with prospective buyers.* This gentleman's bad luck turned out to be £20 million worth of good luck. This is a true story, look it up on Google.

So now you know you can control your luck to an extent. You don't need lucky charms, you just need a positive attitude, a relaxed outlook on life, a belief in your gut feelings, and to be open to speaking to new people and trying new things.

FINDING LEADS AND
SPOTTING OPPORTUNITIES

This section of the book has me very excited. I love spotting opportunities. I love spotting opportunities because at first I never knew how to find them. Recruitment is always easier when you call a client who's recruiting, or when they're getting ready to recruit. In this section of the book I'll show you how to find leads and spot opportunities.

1. **Cold calling:** yes, you already know this one, but the more telephone calls you make the more opportunities you're likely to come across.

2. **Candidate calls:** your candidates are your direct link with your competitors and the job market. They'll be put forward for roles by other recruitment agencies and be applying for roles directly. Ensure you ask your candi-

dates what roles they're been put forward for so you can identify new leads.

3. **Jobs boards:** there are certain job boards that collate and display all the job adverts online. These will not only show jobs being advertised directly by companies hiring, but also adverts put up by your competitors. When you find a company that's hiring use the information in the job advert to do a strong spec call. Also review your competitors job adverts to see if you can identify if any of your prospect clients are recruiting through them.

4. **Newspaper adverts:** some companies still use newspapers to advertise for roles. Scan through newspapers each morning to see if there are any opportunities to chase.

5. **Newspapers and online news:** Scan through relevant newspapers and online news websites, especially the business sections. If you read about companies being setup, moving onto your patch or going into administration, these are all opportunities for you.

6. **LinkedIn:** companies now advertise their vacancies on LinkedIn. They can do this in a number of ways. They can do it through an official job posting, they can do it through their LinkedIn company page, or they can get their employees do to a newsfeed update. Follow companies on LinkedIn and connect

with your clients. Every morning and lunch-time look through your LinkedIn newsfeed to spot any opportunities.

7. **Social media:** a lot of companies now post their vacancies on social media platforms. Follow your clients on these platforms and check if they're recruiting.

8. **Company websites:** check the websites of you clients regularly, because they'll advertise roles they're recruiting for. Use this information to do a spec call.

What other things can you do to spot opportunities and find leads?

OBJECTION HANDLING AND PREFERRED SUPPLIERS

Before I go into objection handling I've a sneaking suspicion that you've skipped every other section and gone straight to this one. Great! You're using this book how I intended, and I would've done exactly the same. If you're in the bookstore and you've spotted this book and you've decided to read this section, buy the book. If it teaches you one thing and that results in a placement, then you'll have a return on investment that far outweighs the cost.

Okay let's get back on topic. An objection is when a client finds a legitimate reason, or just any reason, not to do business with you. Sometimes it's just to get you off the telephone, and sometimes they do it to test you.

Objection handling is a skill used by a recruitment

consultant to reassure the client, demonstrate their unique selling point and build rapport.

To successfully handle objections every recruiter will need:

- An opportunistic approach
- A stock of questions and answers
- A natural instinctive response

THE OBJECTION HANDLING APPROACH

Objections come with the job, and they can be terrifying to some recruitment consultants. Of course, you're being rejected and you're being rejected in such a way that you have to come back with an intelligent and sharp answer.

So how do you currently feel about objections? Write them down and don't read on until you have your answers.

This is important, so I hope you wrote them down. If you haven't, please do so. You'll get more out of this exercise if you do.

What did you write? If you're like most recruitment consultants then you'll have put: frustrating, irritating, disheartening, they're a road block, they put me on the spot and clients say "every recruiter says that."

The problem here is that these are negative feelings towards objections. These feelings are going to prevent you from picking up the phone. They're going to affect the tonality of your voice and your ability to think on your feet.

Now if you ask a successful recruiter how they feel about objections they'll tell you that they're "opportunities" to stand out from their competitors. They're "opportunities" to show the client how sharp they are. In fact, they like objections, otherwise they might as well be in a transactional sales role.

Have another look at your list and be honest with yourself. Do you feel negatively towards objections, or were they more aligned with those of a successful recruiter?

If they're positive, great: you're on your way to being a successful recruiter. If they were negative, no problem, that's why you've bought this book. All you need to do is change the way you look at objections. This isn't some psychological rubbish, this is genuine stuff. For example, most people would look on a derelict building in a rundown area as an eye sore and a waste of space. They couldn't imagine anyone wanting to use it in any way. However, these places can be gold mines, and some very famous property tycoons have made a lot of money by converting such locations into beautiful places for people to enjoy. It's their ability to see opportunity and good in the things most people see as bad.

So the first thing you're going to do is change your mind set. Objection handling is an opportunity for you to play chess with your client. It's an opportunity for you to outsmart your competitors and demonstrate to your client how sharp you are. Objections are there to keep out the recruiters who want quick wins, who don't study sales material and who don't want it bad enough. The thrill of getting past objections and placing a candidate is an amazing feeling.

The second thing you're going to do is manage your own expectations. Only in a few cases will a client let you recruit for them on the first call. In most cases, even if you handle the objections of a client like a seasoned professional, it doesn't guarantee that they'll let you recruit for them there and then. They may not be recruiting or they may be near the end of recruiting. The important thing to know is that when you handle objections well you'll get on their radar and go up a level.

The third thing you're going to do is relax. An objection can knock you off your advancement like a left hook from Mike Tyson. This is when you might start stuttering or saying anything to fill the gap while you think of something intelligent to say. When you face an objection, take a deep breath. This is simply to keep you relaxed so you can think on your feet and implement your objection handling training.

The fourth thing you're going to do is become familiar with common objections. Then we're going to create and memorise stock answers to these objections. To win a game of poker, you need better cards than your competition, or you need to make them think that you do. To overcome objections you'll need questions and answers that'll help trump the client's objection. Most people, unless they're a genius, or very experienced, won't be able to do this from the top of their head. Most people need a stock of answers they can draw upon.

The fifth thing we're going to do is practice objection handling. When you watch a fight, or a football game, the sports professional doesn't think: *There's an opening I'll take a shot.* Instead, their body reacts instantaneously to the opportunity. Another example is blinking. If something unexpectedly comes towards your eyes you don't think: *Oh no there's something coming to my eyes I must shut my eyes.* You do it instinctively. An amazing thing about the human body is that you can train it to develop these instincts. To do this you need to practice the same thing over and over again until your muscles develop muscle memory and it becomes natural. If you want to be natural at objection handling, all you need to do is practice.

Now I know you're itching for the tangible lines that'll knock objections out of the park. We'll discuss these in the next section.

COMMON OBJECTIONS

In this section, I'll present lists of questions and answers to overcome objections. These are general and I recommend and urge you to personalise them to reflect your unique selling points. They're not in any particular order and you wouldn't be expected to say every line to your client.

"Recruitment agencies are too expensive"

Firstly, acknowledge the objection: "Okay, that's good. Understandably saving money is important to you. My ambition is to save you time and money."

1. Do you have an in house recruiter? No, have you worked out how much it costs to take you / one of your staff away from their day job to recruit?
2. If you look at what we do, we actually save

you money. We put up the adverts; we vet, reference and interview the candidates; and if you don't hire any of the candidates it's cost you nothing.

3. How do you normally recruit?

4. Why don't we compare the cost of my services vs. your current method, how would you feel if I could save you money and time?

5. How long does it normally take you to fill vacancies?

6. What would you do if one of your staff goes on long term sickness, or maternity leave?"

7. It doesn't cost you anything to try our services. Why don't you let me send you two CV's and see what you think?

"We have no budget left at the moment"

Firstly acknowledge the objection: "Okay, that's not a problem."

1. To be honest with you, this gives us an opportunity to get to know each other. I'd like to understand your business more, so when you do need to recruit I can react fast for you.

2. Out of curiosity, when is your budget renewed?

3. How much do you normally budget for recruitment?

4. What time of the year do you usually run out of budget?

5. What would you do if one of your staff goes on long term sickness, or maternity leave?"

"It's company policy not to use agencies"
Firstly acknowledge the objection: "Oh okay."

1. How do you normally recruit?
2. What was the reason for the policy? (Money? Bad experience?)
3. How are you managing your current recruitment methods?
4. How successful are your current recruitment methods?
5. Have you ever tried an agency before?
6. When do you expect this situation to change? (record this and chase)
7. How long has the policy been in place?
8. What calibre of candidates does your current recruitment method find?
9. What type of staff do you find recruiting difficult for?
10. What would you do if one of your staff goes on long term sickness, or maternity leave?"

"There's a recruitment freeze"
Firstly acknowledge the objection: "Oh that's a shame, I've heard you're a good company to work for."

1. What's the reason for the freeze?
2. When do you expect it will pass? (record this and chase)
3. When do you think you'll be recruiting again?
4. I understand you have a freeze. How is this affecting you and your department?
5. What would you do if one of your staff goes on long term sickness, or maternity leave?"
6. How is this affecting your job?
7. What would happen if you lost a key member of staff, how would you go about replacing them?

"We advertise ourselves" (newspaper / website)

Firstly acknowledge the objection: "I understand."

1. Where do you advertise?
2. If an advert costs you £2000, but doesn't find the right candidate, what do you do then?
3. Most of my clients used to advertise themselves until they gave me a chance. With my services you don't pay until you hire the candidate. Next time, why don't you give me a chance before paying for an advert? If it doesn't work out you've lost nothing
4. How successful is your advertising?
5. How much do you spend on advertising?
6. Who deals with the responses?

7. How much does sifting through all those CV's take you away from your day job?
8. What's the calibre of candidates who respond?
9. What do you do if you don't get the right response?
10. What would you do if you needed someone immediately?
11. I can complement what you're already doing. If you advertise and use me at the same time then you can compare what I'm sending you to what your advert attracts.

"We only use large agencies that can fill multiple roles"

Firstly acknowledge the objection: "I can see the sense in that. That probably makes it easier than dealing with multiple agencies."

1. Many of my clients previously only used large generalist agencies, but they found they weren't getting the top candidates. They simply can't keep on top of every profession.
2. Large agencies have to hide candidates from their clients, because it would mean headhunting candidates from their other clients. They wouldn't do this for ethical reasons. With so many clients they can't headhunt candidates for you. I only work with a select

few clients, so I actually have a bigger pool of candidates for you.

"We use another agency"

Firstly acknowledge the objection: "I'm glad to see that you take recruitment seriously."

1. What agency do you use?
2. How did they get to work with you?
3. What is the reason for using them?
4. What is it about their service you prefer?
5. What other agencies do you use as back up?
6. What types of staff do they supply you with?
7. What do you do if they can't deliver?
8. Would you ever go out to another agency if needed?
9. What do you look for in a recruitment agency?
10. What could they do to improve?
11. What would you change about their current service?
12. I really want to work with your company. What can I do to get that opportunity?

"Your fees are too expensive"

Firstly acknowledge the objection: "That's why you should use me."

1. I charge more because I go the extra mile. I deliver a premium service and you'll only ever get two to three CV's of interviewed, referenced and relevant candidates. If I can't deliver, I'll honestly tell you straight away rather than waste your time.

"We're not recruiting right now"

Firstly acknowledge the objection: "That's not a problem."

1. I'm interested in your company and while there is nothing happening now, I genuinely want to know you and understand your business for when you do recruit.
2. What do you normally do when you are recruiting?
3. When do you think you'll next be recruiting?
4. I read that your company is planning on growing, how do you expect your department to change with this growth?
5. I read that your company is considering a stock market floatation. What recruitment measure are you taking for this change?
6. I'm glad you're currently not recruiting. This is gives me an opportunity to better understand your business.

"We don't use recruitment agencies"

Firstly acknowledge the objection: "Oh okay."

1. How come you don't use agencies?
2. How do you employ temporary workers?
3. How do you keep productivity up when spreading staff duties?
4. How do you cover staff?
5. How do you pay temporary staff?
6. What happens if one of your employees goes on sick leave or maternity?
7. How do you recruit for specialist skill sets?
8. How do you cover peak trading periods?
9. What issues do you face when people leave or go on leave?

"It's my job – Internal recruitment"

Firstly acknowledge the objection: "Great I'm speaking to the right person."

1. I believe your company has 2000 employees, that must be hard to manage, what external support do you use?
2. Who covers you when you're ill or taking holidays?
3. What do you know about recruitment agencies?
4. How often do you recruit?
5. What candidates do you find hard to find?
6. How would you feel about partnering with an

agency and using our facilities for private discreet interviews?

7. What do you look for in an agency?
8. Which positions are the most difficult to fill?
9. Who does the interviews?
10. What do you do if you can't find the right candidates?

"I've had problems with your agency in the past"

Firstly acknowledge the objection: "I'm sorry to hear that. That's really frustrating."

1. What happened?
2. When did this happen?
3. What was done to solve the issue?
4. Who did you talk to?
5. What can I do to leave you with a better taste?
6. What areas were you happy with?
7. I want to fix this for you, what would you need?
8. How can I help you?

"We currently making redundancies"

Firstly acknowledge the objection: "I'm sorry to hear that. I'd love to help."

1. I can come to your offices and help your staff

with CV writing, and how to find their next role. I can also register them and help them find new roles. This will also benefit you as I'll better understand your business. This means I can help you for when business picks up and you quickly need to find staff.

"I'm too busy to talk"

Firstly acknowledge the objection: "No problem."

1. When would be a better time to call you back?
2. I'm keen to work with you, when would be a good time to talk?

"I can't talk just send me some CV's"

Firstly acknowledge the objection: "I'm glad you want me to send you some CV's."

1. In order for me to give you a professional service I would need to know more about the role and exactly what you're looking for. I would never just send any CV, I send relevant CV's. When would be a better time to talk?

In section two we discussed Neil Rackham's SPIN® selling. Refer back to this section specifically on need-payoff questions. Rackham found that need-payoff questions reduce objections from clients. This is because need-payoff questions flip the selling. Now instead the client explains to you what problems your services can solve for them, so they are selling to you how you can help them. In other words they find the benefits of your services through your questioning and then tell you them. As a result they find the solution more acceptable.

PREFERRED SUPPLIER LIST (PSL)

A preferred supplied list, also known as a PSL, is exactly what it says. It's a list of suppliers who the client prefers to use. I've decided to give this topic a section of its own, because I've seen recruitment consultants become unnecessarily frustrated and disheartened by the words "PSL".

If you're just starting up a new recruitment desk you'll probably hear the term preferred supplier list a lot, as most of your clients, especially the larger organisations, will have one. Don't view a company with a PSL as an impenetrable castle. See it as a positive. See it as an opportunity to accomplish a goal, to grow your skills and develop your character. Firstly, the company uses recruitment agencies, so that's a plus. Secondly, it's an opportunity to send CV's that beat the CV's provided by the suppliers on their PSL. Thirdly, once you're on the PSL you'll know it will discourage recruitment consultants who don't have the right skills, the right training and the tenacity to get on it.

To a skilled and determined recruitment consultant a PSL is not worth the paper it's written on. At the end of the day a PSL is just a piece of paper. Imagine you were your client with a PSL in place. Then a recruitment agency who wasn't on your PSL sent you a CV that was better than all the CV's provided by your preferred suppliers. You would have no choice but to work with that agency and see that candidate.

There are several ways to break through a PSL. The first way is to play the long game: to treat the client like they don't have a PSL. Keep the company on your monthly call list and your monthly e-shot list. Keep sending to them and talking to them about high-calibre industry-related candidates. They'll soon realise you're a smart, intelligent recruitment consultant. An example of a conversation could be:

You: "Hi Tony, It's <your name> from <your company>. How are you?"

Client: "Hi, as I've said before we've got a PSL in place."

You: "I know and I completely respect that you do. However, I had to run this candidate past you. She's moving into the area and she currently works for a competitor of yours called Automotive Cars. You've heard of them right?"

Client: "Yes."

You: "She was part of the team that launched the new energy efficient car. She's relocating up North due to family commitments and she's only working with me. I thought you might be interested in her CV?"

Client: "Okay."

You: "I'll send you over her CV now."

The second way, which is how I broke into my patch, is through hard-to-recruit-for positions. There'll be occasions when the client wants a difficult and hard to find candidate. The suppliers on the PSL will immediately jump into action to find the client this candidate, but eventually their energy will run out as they struggle to find the right candidate. They'll make a business decision to concentrate on filling the roles of other clients, which will be easier to place. Meanwhile the client becomes frustrated with their preferred suppliers and loses faith in them. This is when you come in and offer a solution to the client's problem. If you're new to recruitment and you don't have many clients you're more likely to fill these placements. As a result, your client will see you as a hero and they'll put you at the top of the PSL, running any new vacancies past you first.

An important point is to always sell to the MAN, which stands for 'money, authority and need'. The MAN can be male or female, but they're the line managers of the company. Unless you're recruiting for HR staff you should avoid HR and sell directly to line managers. The line managers are the people who have the staffing problem. They're the people who know exactly what they want in a candidate and what skills and personality they should have. They also are less precious about the PSL, as they just want the problem solved. If you send the right candidates to the line manager and build up a good relationship with them, they'll push HR on your behalf.

DON'T RELY ON COMMON PSL QUESTIONS

You'll have probably been trained to ask the following questions:

- When are you renewing your PSL?
- Who's on your PSL?
- How did they get on the PSL?
- How do I become a preferred supplier?
- Who owns the PSL?

- What do you look for in a recruitment agency?
- What's your back up plan if your suppliers can't deliver?
- When was the last time you had to go outside of the PSL?
- What do you like about those agencies on your PSL?
- How could they make your current service better?
- How can I become a second tier supplier?

While these are good questions and they do have a place, a company isn't going to put you on their PSL if you haven't recruited for them before. Unfortunately, you won't be given the opportunity to recruit for them, because you're not on the PSL. It's a bit like the chicken and the egg paradox.

Therefore, the best way to get on a PSL is to be disruptive. Use the two strategies above. Ignore the PSL and keep sending high-calibre candidates to the line manager. When you see an opportunity where the client is struggling, take full advantage by becoming their hero. PSL's become less of a problem the longer you're in recruitment. The reason for this is simply because you get to know your patch well enough to spec good candidates in, and your competitors will make mistakes the longer they're on the PSL.

PART 3

THE RECRUITMENT SALES METHODOLOGY

In part three, I'll discuss a step-by-step methodology to recruitment. It'll take the principles of sales and apply them to recruitment. Something I desperately wanted access to when I started out.

As I talk you through each stage I'll use an example, when appropriate, based on my experience as a specialist finance recruitment consultant, so the example at times will relate to finance. However, the methods used are generally similar regardless of the industry you work in, but please do tailor them to suit your audience.

Cold Calling In Recruitment

INTRODUCTION CALL – YOUR FIRST CALL

Your introductory call is the first time you speak to your client. Funnily enough, on your first call you're not going to sell anything. Instead you're simply going to introduce your details to the client and get their email address. The reason we don't sell at this stage is because you don't have enough information about your client to sell intelligently. In order to sell intelligently you would need to know what type of employees work for them, how many employees work in their department, what computer systems they use, what qualifications they require, along with a great deal of other important information. At the same time, not many people will openly talk to you about their business on your first call. When you're very experienced you'll be able to sell on your first call, using a technique called "speccing". I've mentioned spec calls earlier in the book and we'll discuss them more later, but for now we'll go through a step-by-step method.

Before you make the call do a small amount of research. Enough to make you knowledgeable, but not so much that it takes up too much time. Look on the company's website to establish what they do, what they sell and how big they are. Look on networking websites such as LinkedIn to see the client's profile. This will tell you how long they've been in the company and what their background is. Once you have all this information capture it on your client database. Now in the future a quick scan of your database will tell you everything you need to know, and eventually all this information will store in your memory.

You're now ready to make the call. You might not get through on the first time, or even the second time, which is why you shouldn't plan too much. Once you're through, your first call may go as follows:

You: "Hi, <client name>. We've not spoken before. My name is <your name>. I work for a company called <agency name> and I'm a specialist <industry> recruiter. I'm calling to introduce myself and

<agency name> to you. Do you have an email address so that I can send you my details?

Thank you, I'll send you them now."

That's all you do. You've introduced yourself and you've got a small commitment from them, which is their email address. Now you want to send them an email to provide them with more information and your contact details. You'll also want to attach any company literature to strengthen your creditability. Below is an example of an introductory email you could send.

Hi <name>,

Thank you for your time on the telephone earlier.

As discussed, I am a specialist <industry> recruitment consultant working for a company called <company name>.

<Company name> has been around for X number of years and we offer a tailored and professional recruitment service to our clients.

I have attached a brochure for your information, but you can also find out more by visiting <agency website>.

I will call you in about a week's time to collect your thoughts, but if I can help you beforehand, please, do not hesitate to contact me via telephone on: <number> or via email <email address>

Kind regards

<Your name>

You'll notice in the email I've said you'll call them in a week's time. This initial short time frame between the first call, the email then the second call is important in getting the client to remember you and your company.

Hopefully you've recognised that this is the power of three: first call, email then second call.

SECOND CALL

The aim of the first call is simply to get the relationship going and warm the client up. Now on your second call they will:

- Remember who you are
- Understand why you're calling
- Know your company name and what you do

You're in a much better position than when you first called, and the client is more likely to offer you any current positions they want filling, or provide you with any company information. However, in this case, let's focus on the situation when the client isn't recruiting.

Your second call and any future calls should have a minimum of **three objectives**. This could be to get three pieces of information, for example:

- How many employees are in their team?
- What recruitment agencies do they use?
- What's their direct line?

The information you gather from your three objectives is the information you then use to sell in future calls.

Below is a call script for your second call. Every recruitment consultant, no matter how experienced, should have a call script in front of them. The idea is to sound natural, as if you don't have a call script in front of you, but you should be using one. The way you make your call sound like you're not using a call script is by varying the tonality of your voice, and adapting the conversation to the client's answers.

Notice that the script below is broken into three parts, an introduction, middle and an end.

"Hi <client name>, it's <your name> calling from <agency name>. We spoke on the phone last week.

As you know, I'm keen to work with you and in order for me to run the best candidates past you could you help me by answering a few questions?

- *How many employees are in your team?*
- *What types of employees are in your team?*
- *Which recruitment agencies do you use?*

Thank you for your time, before I go, do you have anything I need to put in my diary for you?"

For simplicity, I've stuck to three questions to hit my three objectives. If the conversation is going well and the client is opening up, I would ask more insightful questions to find further information.

Now let's use the above script in an example, so you can see it in practice. The company is called Hooze Food, which is a food manufacturing company and the decision maker is a Finance Director called Alison Hall.

Me: "Hi Alison, it's Andrew Leong calling from The Rich Recruiter. We spoke last week?"

Alison: "Hello, yes, I remember."

Me: "As you know, I'm keen to work with you and in order for me to run the best candidates past you could you help me by answering a few questions?"

Alison: "Okay."

Me: "How many employees are in your team?"

Alison: "10."

Me: "10, great. What types of employees are in your team?"

Alison: "I have five Management Accountants and five Finance Clerks."

Me: "I see. What qualifications do they have?"

Alison: "All the Management Accountants have a CIMA professional qualification and the Finance Clerks are unqualified."

Me: "Uh-huh, CIMA qualified. And finally, which recruitment agencies do you use?"

Alison: "I use Super Recruitment and Finance Now."

Me: "Great, it's good that you have a recruitment process in place. Thank you for your time, before I go, do you want me to keep an eye out for any candidates for you?"

Alison: "Not at this moment."

Me: "No problem, thanks again, speak to you soon."

Alison: "Bye."

I emphasise that I haven't done any selling on this call, only gathered intelligence for future calls. Let's break the conversation down. Firstly, I reintroduced myself. Secondly, when I respond to the answers of my questions I show the client I'm listening by saying things like "Uh-huh" and "I see" – (see the section on listening). I also demonstrate I'm listening and build credibility by repeating back to the client what they've said. Thirdly, on the last question I say "finally", so the client knows they're not going to be asked a hundred questions. You can only ask a large amount of questions when you're taking down a job specification, or reviewing a candidate, and we're not at that stage yet. Lastly, notice that in the last section of the call I ask if the client would like me to keep an eye out for any candidates. This is a gentle but direct way of asking if they're planning any recruitment actives in the near future. You're more likely to get a response this way rather than asking "when do you next plan to recruit?" As you'll have seen I follow the script, but I don't stick to it 100 percent, instead I adapt to the conversation.

During the conversation I'll have recorded all this information on the client database. In addition to your database, you should produce fact sheets for every important client you prospect. These sheets will contain all the powerful information you collect on a one page summary. An example of a fact sheet is given below.

Client Fact Sheet

Client's Name: *Hooze Food*
Industry: *Food Production*
Decision Maker(s): *Alison Hall*
Title: *Finance Director*
Department Number: *10*
Types of staff: *5 x Management Accountants &*
5 x Finance Clerks
Qualifications: *Management Accountants are CIMA qualified*
Computer Systems:
Financial Year End:
Agencies Used: *'Super Recruitment' and 'Finance Now'*
Preferred Supplier List:

Reasons For These Suppliers:
Last Recruited:
Temps:
Client's Competitors: *Tasty Treats, Super Foods and Delicious Dinners*

You'll have now started to build a picture of the client that enables you to send the right types of candidates. From this information alone we could do an impressive sales call that would boost your credibility with that client. You may have noticed that we have more information to gather. You could gather all this information on your first call, but it all depends on how receptive your client is.

If you can remember back to section two, advanced questioning, you may have noticed that in this call I asked the client only situation questions. We know that by asking too many situation questions clients quickly become bored. However, they're essential at the initial stages to understand your client. At the same time, clients are unlikely to discuss problems with you at this stage until they know you better. One exception to this is when the client is a distressed buyer and they need to buy now. In most cases it's in later telephone calls that you start to ask problem questions, implication questions and needs-pay off questions, such as:

- What problems do you find when recruiting?
- What impact does this have?
- Would you find my services useful if I could solve this problem?

THIRD CALL – SPECCING CALL & SALES CALL

On your third call you're now ready to start selling, and we'll use the information gathered from the second call to do the selling. One of the most difficult parts of cold calling in recruitment is that you don't have a tangible product to sell. Imagine you're walking through a fruit market and a seller shouts you over to look at their empty stall. You ask the seller what they're selling and they say, apples. Confused you reply "but your stall is empty?" The seller says "I can go and get whatever apple you want." Meanwhile the seller on the stall next door is offering you a delicious mouth-watering apple. You can see it, touch it and smell it. Who are you going to buy from?

Cold calling and asking the client if they're recruiting isn't going to get you far. You won't have the excitement, passion and tonality in your voice that gets the client excited. You also won't be offering them any solutions to problems they're having. To solve this situation you need a product, but not just any product, a product that your client would want. Your product comes in the form of a high-calibre candidate. This is called a speccing call or a spec call.

Firstly, you need a great candidate to sell. Sticking with our example of Alison Hall at Hooze Foods, from our research and from the first telephone call with her we know she hires qualified CIMA Management Accountants and Finance Clerks. The organisation is in the food production industry and she uses recruitment agencies.

You would now look for candidates who fitted this picture. You would find a candidate who was CIMA qualified or studying, had management accounting experience and who had worked in food production, manufacturing or fast moving consumer goods (FMCG). What if you don't have a candidate to use for a speccing in call? When rich recruiters can't find a candidate with the relevant qualities, they simply make the candidate up, I'll explain this later.

For the purpose of this demonstration let's say we've found a candidate who matches these qualities. You'll need to have at least telephone interviewed this candidate. You'll also need to prepare their CV to send to the client after the telephone conversation.

Before the telephone conversation, prepare a short sharp, snappy script based on the power of three. Pick three strong points from the candidate's CV and from something you discovered from interviewing the candidate. All these points need to match what the client would look for in a candidate.

In the case of Hooze Foods, the three points could be:

1. CIMA qualified Management Accountant
2. Background in food production
3. Successfully saved £500K last year through process improvement

The first two points demonstrate to Alison that I've listened to what she said. This is what builds trust and a reputation as an intelligent recruitment consultant. The third point I've selected is a quantifiable achievement. A quantifiable achievement is far more powerful and persuasive than saying something along the lines of "They're a great manager". The number makes it more real and measurable.

As before, make a script:

"Hi <client name>, it's <your name>, from a <your company>. We spoke last month.

I'd like to run a candidate past you I think you'd be interested in.

1. *They're a CIMA qualified Management Accountant*
2. *Their background is in food production*
3. *They successfully saved £500K last year through improving the company's processes.*

How does this candidate sound to you?"

There are several ways this conversation could end up going, but I'll concentrate on two possible scenarios:

1. The client is not interested
2. The client is recruiting

Now let's use this in our example, so you can see it in practice. Firstly, in this example we'll concentrate on the situation when the client isn't interested.

Me: "Hi Alison, it's Andrew Leong, from The Rich Recruiter. We spoke last month."

Alison: "Okay."

Me: "I'd like to run a candidate past you I think you'd be interested in.

- They're a CIMA qualified Management Accountant
- Their background's in food production working at your competitor Tasty Treats
- They successfully saved £500K last year through improving the company's processes

How does this candidate sound to you?"

Alison: "We're not recruiting at the moment."

Me: "No problem, I'll inform the candidate for you. Do you mind me asking if this is the type of candidate that interests you?

Alison: "Yes, they sound good."

Me: "Okay that's good. While I've got you on the phone, do you mind me asking what software systems you use?"

Alison: "We use SAP."

Me: "Great. Out of curiosity when do you use temporary staff?"

Alison: "To cover maternity or shortages in staff."

Me: "I see. Do you have any temps in at the moment?"

Alison: "Yes, we have two finance clerks through Super Recruitment."

Me: "How do you find working with Super Recruitment?"

Alison: "They're fine."

Me: "If you don't mind me asking, if you could improve their service in any area what would it be?"

Alison: "Nothing at the moment. They're doing a good job."

Me: "That's good to know. Well thank you very much for your time on the telephone. Before I go do you want me to put anything in the diary for you?

Even though the client wasn't buying I kept asking open questions to identify more information about the client's situation. Now from this conversation I know they use the software system SAP, they have temporary staff and they have them through the agency Super Recruitment. I can use this information to help me sell again in the future, especially candidates who have experience in SAP. At the same time I'll have increased my reputation by speccing in a relevant candidate. I've used an example were the client is being closed off, even though I'm asking relevant questions. I've done this to demonstrate that relationship building is a timely process and you will come up against many clients who won't give you a chance at first. Your clients are called daily by many recruitment agencies, so you've got to stand out from the crowd. You do this by taking your time, being professional, taking the client with you, and demonstrating your recruitment ability.

Don't fall into the trap that if you don't close a deal on every phone call you're doing a bad job. This is simply not true or practical. If a department isn't hiring, it's not hiring, no matter what you say. Trying to force a client to buy a candidate is bad sales, and will do nothing but damage your reputation.

I would now follow up the telephone call with a polite email with the CV attached. State in the email that you did listen on the telephone and that you know they're not currently recruiting, but it might be a CV they want to file away for future vacancies. The reason for this email is simply marketing and to show the client how good your candidates are. They'll look at the CV, even if they're not recruiting. People are naturally curious so in most cases they'll look. Also, an email received after a telephone call helps to embed your name and company name within the client's mind. Therefore, you start to get on their radar as a good recruitment consultant and they'll think of you when they do recruit.

The alternative situation is when you call, and the client is recruiting. For example:

Alison: "We're recruiting at the moment, but that's not what we're looking for."

Me: "Oh you're currently in the market? What type of candidate are you looking for?"

This leads into the next section, which we'll arrive at shortly.

After your second call to a client most of your calls should be speccing calls. It involves finding a good, relevant candidate and selling them to your client. Then using the telephone call to ask the client further questions.

When searching for candidates always keep in mind your clients. Keep asking yourself, where would this candidate be a good fit?

Being an experienced recruiter I understand that finding good candidates for every one of your clients is time consuming, and ultimately impossible. Earlier, I explained that rich recruiters make candidates up. Initially this may sound scary and wrong, but it's an extremely powerful technique. It also benefits the client, because they'll start to favour you over other recruitment consultants, and you're the best person for the job, right? The goal isn't for clients to buy the made up candidate, but to show them you're sharp, you've listened and you understand them. It's also to get the client to open up and provide you with more information or tell you about any vacancies they're recruiting for.

Using the example of Hooze Foods I could have easily made up a candidate. In fact, I did make that candidate up and it took me about 30 seconds.

The reason you can do this is because you've formed an understanding of the client's needs through your second call and your research. They say information is power, but it's only powerful if you use it effectively. You have the information so use it.

Once you've specced in your candidate, if the client isn't currently recruiting you simply put in your diary to call them next month. If the client is recruiting, great, you're now going to learn how to handle this in the next section.

TAKING A JOB
SPECIFICATION

A vacancy can arise from a telephone call, an e-shot or an email you've sent, or the client can call you; whatever the method, the process for capturing the details of the vacancy is the same.

You need to know the following:

Client Details

- Who's in charge of the recruitment for this particular vacancy? - *It could be a different person from the telephone call*
- Which company is hiring? – *If they have called in, you need to make sure you get the name of the company*
- What's their direct telephone number, and mobile number? – *You don't have time to deal*

with gatekeepers and this is an ideal time to get their direct number

- What's the address of the site that the candidate will be based at? – *The vacancy could be at a different site*

Vacancy Details

- What's the job title?
- When do you need them to start?
- What is the salary?
- Is there any flexibility on the salary?
- Who will they be reporting to?
- What's the structure of the department / team?
- What are the daily duties?
- Why has this vacancy come about? – *If it's due to growth, then you know there could be more opportunities soon.*
- How big is the team/department the candidate will be working in?
- What is the company/department culture like?
- How many CV's do they want?
- When do they want CV's by / what is the deadline for CV's?
- What benefits come with the role? (car park, flexible hours, healthcare)

Process Details

- What's the recruitment process for this position?
- Following a CV submission, when would they give feedback?
- When are they planning on interviewing?
- How many are they planning on interviewing?
- We'll go through more about the client's recruitment and interview process later in the book.

Candidate Details

- What software skills do they need to have?
- What industry background should they ideally come from?
- What qualifications do they need?
- Does the candidate need to drive or need a car?
- What skills does the candidate need (essential / desirable)?
- What type of personality should they have?
- What was the personality of the previous employee?

Competitor Details

- Who else is working on this vacancy?
- Are there any other agencies working on this vacancy? Which?
- How long have you been recruiting for this position?

- What CV's / candidates have you seen already? *- get the names of candidates to avoid duplication*
- What did you like about them? How could they be improved?
- Do you have any internal people applying for the job?

While this may look like a lot of questions, they're extremely important. The client will understand what you're doing and will find the time to go through the answers with you.

The answers to these questions enable you to search for the exact candidate your client is looking for, or at least a close match. It will also aid you in writing a job advert that'll attract the best candidates.

Remembering all these questions from the top of your head is a difficult task, even for an experienced recruiter. Therefore, it's best to always have on top of your desk a stack of **job specifications**. A job specification is a form that you complete while on the phone to the client and it has many purposes:

1. It reminds you of which questions to ask
2. It becomes your reference point when searching for candidates and creating job adverts
3. It provides you with a massive amount of

information regarding your client that you can refer to in the future

If you're not using a job specification form you can download one for free from therichrecruiter.com. You may brand this and use this as your own.

As you go through the job specification questions, when you reach the question: "Are there any other agencies working on this vacancy?" if the client replies "no" You should ask for **exclusivity** for the vacancy and offer them a reduced fee rate in return. If they're reluctant, ask for exclusivity for a time period of a week or a few days. Even one day can be enough to put you ahead of the competition. Exclusivity of a vacancy means that you'll be the only recruitment company recruiting for the vacancy. This is highly beneficial, because all recruitment companies are generally trading candidates from the same labour market. Exclusivity will enable you to secure candidates' CV's and get them to your client before your competition does. Like all sales you'll need to sell the benefits of exclusivity, for example:

You: "Can you leave this vacancy just with me and I'll give you a reduced rate? It'll also mean you won't have to spend all day speaking to other recruitment agencies."

As discussed earlier in the book some clients may want to discuss fee rates before the job specification and some will near the end of the specification. Refer back to the section on negotiating. Remember you're trying to create a win-win situation for you and the client.

Clients will have in their head exactly the type of person they're after, and this can sometimes be unrealistic. It's important that you ask your client to flex the specification, which means widening the options they'll consider. You should ask questions such as:

- What's the most important thing to you that the candidate must have?
- What's the least important?
- What can go from this specification if needed?
- Would you consider a candidate from a different industry?
- Would you consider looking at candidates who live outside the area?

Once you've ended the call you'll want to prioritise the job specification through a classification system such as 1, 2 and 3. If the position is extremely hard to recruit for and the candidate supply is low you might mark this as a three and put it to the back of your list. If the position is a hot job, the candidate supply is strong and the client needs an immediate start. Then you could class this with a one for being urgent.

HOW TO TRANSITION FROM A SPEC CALL TO A JOB IN CALL

In the previous section we left the conversation as follows:

Alison: "We're recruiting at the moment, but that's not what we're looking for."

Me: "What type of candidate are you looking for?"

Alison: "I'm looking for a CIMA qualified Management Accountant."

Me: (close and transition) "Let me take some details down from you, so I can serve you better."

It's at this point I'll go straight to my job specification and start asking the questions which are on the form.

Also in the previous section I discussed the technique of creating a fictional candidate for your spec call. No doubt you'll feel quite apprehensive about this especially if you think the client will respond positively to your fictional candidate. I'll demonstrate how you solve this.

Alison: "They sound good, that's what I'm looking for at the moment."

Me: "Oh great, so you're currently looking?"

Alison: "Yes."

Me: (close and transition) "Okay, let me take some details down from you first to ensure there's a good match."

After you have taken the job specification:

Me: "Now I've got all the details I don't think this particular candidate is the best person. However, I do have a couple of other candidates in mind for you. I'll send you their CV's as soon as possible."

RECONFIRM THE JOB SPECIFICATION

One of the best ways to build trust with a client and have them feel confident in you is to reconfirm everything back with the client. You do this by summarising back what they've told you, for example:

You: "So you want a CIMA qualified Management Accountant?"

Client: "Yes."

You: "And you want them to have experience of communicating with clients?"

Client: "Yes."

You: "And you need CV's by Friday?"

Client: "Yes."

Not only does this show the client you've listened, it will enable you to correct the specification if you've misunderstood anything. This leaves the client confident that you understand their needs, but it also leaves you confident that you have all the correct information.

Searching For
Candidates

Once you've completed your job specification with your client and you're absolutely sure you have all the details you'll want to begin your search. Recruitment is a fast paced environment and if you don't secure your candidates first your competitors will. This is another fun part of recruitment and often why late nights come with the job.

So what are the methods of finding candidates and what order should you do them in? In this section I'll describe both the methods you should use and the order you should use them, but you may change this order depending on your industry and your company's culture.

Shout Outs

A shout out should be your first method. This simply involves shouting out in the office to your colleagues that you have a job on, and asking if they can recommend some candidates.

This method largely depends on the culture of the recruitment agency. Some recruitment agencies are highly cut-throat and internally competitive. In these environments your colleagues may not be willing to help you and they may not be putting good candidates on the database. Instead they will keep them in their desk in what is known as 'top drawing'. Such a culture is damaging to clients, candidates, and the recruitment industry alike. It'll also drive good recruiters out of the company and into more professional ones. However, if you work for a good company your colleagues will be willing to recommend you a good candidate they've recently been in contact with or worked with. In some agencies they split the fee with the consultant who found the candidate.

Hot Candidates List
You should keep a list of good candidates that stand out to you and your colleagues, who are immediately available for work. Put this list on the wall in the office for all to see. Refer to this list and see if any of them match your job specification.

Candidate Database
The company you work for should have a database

of candidates that allows you to search by certain criteria. A database is only as good as the information that's been input. Therefore, it is essential that you and your colleagues keep the database up-to-date, complete and comprehensive.

Databases will be different across recruitment agencies, so it would be impossible to explain a one size fits all approach. However, covering the basics, use the location of the client you're recruiting for to search in an outward radius from there. Also use key criteria from your job specification to narrow down your search.

Jobs Board

Some recruitment agencies have a recruitment resourcer whose job is to search for candidates. A good resourcer is worth their weight in gold and if you have access to one, ask them to search the job boards while you search your company database. This will save you a great amount of time. If you don't have access to a resourcer your next method is to search job boards. Job boards are an online database of candidates. You can use them to advertise your jobs or search for candidates.

At the time of writing, all job boards are slightly different, but they all work in very much the same way. You'll be able to search for candidates based on the location and criteria you collected in your job specification.

Search jobs boards that are relevant to the position you're recruiting for first. Only if they don't produce a candidate should you widen your search to less relevant job boards.

LinkedIn

At the time of writing LinkedIn has grown in popularity and has become an essential tool for a recruitment consultant. Surprisingly, not all recruitment consultants have adapted to the times and adopted the use of LinkedIn to its full potential. Some managers who are old school and have been institutionalised may see LinkedIn as a waste of time.

LinkedIn is a massive network of candidates and clients. At the time of writing there were 300,000,000 users with two new members creating a profile every second. (http://press.linkedin.com/about)

The problem with job boards is that not everyone uses them, especially if they're not looking for a job. These candidates are known as **passive candidates**. However, in the age of social networks more and more people will continue to create professional LinkedIn profiles. These profiles are very similar to a CV and they can be used to review and contact candidates about vacancies that you're recruiting for.

LinkedIn has a search function that you can use to search for candidates. Use the location and criteria from your job specification to find the right candidate. Google can also be used to search for candidates on LinkedIn if LinkedIn's search function isn't proving you with satisfactory results. For some technical reason unknown to me, LinkedIn seems to limit basic search criteria on Google. However, you can use the below code to force Google to search LinkedIn more thoroughly:

> *site:uk.linkedin.com* "city, *country" (inurl:in OR inurl:pub) -intitle:directory -inurl:dir -inurl:jobs ("job title") AND ("qualification" OR "skill")*

Copy and paste the above into Google but change the words in the speech marks to suit your needs. For example:

> *site:uk.linkedin.com "london, United Kingdom" (inurl:in OR inurl:pub) -intitle:directory -inurl:dir -inurl:jobs ("Management Accountant") AND ("ACCA" OR "CIMA")*

Notice this sophisticated search syntax can also be used to search for clients to call. Once you find a candidate you're interested in you must connect with them before you can see their contact details. LinkedIn will ask you "How do you know this person?" I've always found the option "We've done business together" to be the most relevant option and then write them a brief and personalised message, such as:

Hi Abigail

I'm currently recruiting for a role that I think you may be interested in.

I'd like to add you to my professional network on LinkedIn and run it past you.

- Andrew Leong

Sometimes candidates just accept your connection without reading your message. Therefore, they fail to reply to you about the vacancy. If a candidate accepts your request but does not reply, be proactive and call them. If they've not put their phone number on their LinkedIn profile send them a message about the vacancy asking for their telephone number and when would be a good time to speak.

What if they do not accept or reply? Some candidates do not check their LinkedIn often or their personal email. Some candidates may simply ignore your connection request. Never assume and never wait too long for a response. Look at their profile to see what company they currently work for and call them at work. This is called **Headhunting**. They will not be able to speak at work, so be sensitive to their situation. Speak to them briefly about why you're calling and ask them for a personal telephone number to contact them after work.

I recommend that you do not headhunt candidates who are working for your clients, especially if you have built up a relationship with the client. This would destroy the relationship if they found out.

There might be a situation in which if you don't headhunt a particular candidate who's working for your client or prospect client then your competitor will. In this case I'll leave it up to your judgement. If you do need to headhunt a candidate from your client or prospect clients, then be very discreet. Candidates are likely to tell their managers that you have called them, because they want their managers to know and feel that they're a valuable asset. In one situation when I called a candidate they shouted very loudly: "No I don't want a new job thank you for calling me", in what I can only imagine was a small show to impress the people around them. Therefore, as an extra precaution, when you headhunt a candidate at their work place just say you're a headhunter and you would like to speak to them after work. Then stay silent to gauge their response. This protects your identify in case the candidate does not want to give you their details and then shouts across their office floor that they're currently being headhunted.

Referrals

There will be times especially in a market with a candidate shortage that you may struggle to find the right candidate. As you speak to candidates who aren't interested in the role ask them if they know anyone who might be interested. They may have a colleague, friend or family member whose looking, but not put themselves on the market yet. You may offer them cash rewards or other incentives if their referred candidate successfully places.

Job Advert

The purpose of a job advert is to attract the best candidates to the role. I have this last on the list for several reasons. Firstly, you have to create the job advert and then upload it to the relevant websites, which can take up valuable time depending on how fast you are. Secondly, it also requires candidates to proactively submit their CV's, which is out of your control. Candidates may be in work or have commitments, so they're unlikely to respond to the job advert during working hours. Consequently, as time is of the essence, use the first five methods first. Then at the end of the day create and upload your job advert, so it can do the work for you while you're away from the office. You should expect to come into the office the next morning to an inbox of candidates, depending on the candidate market.

Writing attractive job adverts is an essential and powerful tool in a recruitment consultant's toolbox. Good job adverts can attract good candidates, and good candidates place vacancies. Therefore, the next section of this book is dedicated to writing job adverts and helping you become an expert.

WRITING JOB ADVERTS

As previously stated writing attractive job adverts is an essential and powerful tool. You must be good at writing job adverts to attract top talent. Even if you have access to a recruitment resourcer I recommend you get into the habit of practicing the art of writing good job adverts. One day you're likely to be in a situation where your resourcer isn't available and you'll have to write job adverts for yourself.

For some recruitment consultants writing job adverts can be a difficult task, especially new recruitment consultants. Writing job adverts is a different sell and a different skill from cold calling, because it requires written sales skills. However, some recruiters love to express themselves in written form, so they find this an enjoyable part of the job.

With the right method, practice and experience

your job adverts will improve dramatically. The time you take to produce them will lessen and they will attract the best candidates.

The job advert must first grasp the attention of the candidate; spark an interest for them to read further and then persuade them to apply. To write effective job adverts you must understand what attracts candidates to apply for roles. Money is not always the main motivation. People are also attracted to sector, industry, company benefits, location, culture, opportunities and other things. You must sell all of these in your job advert, not just the role.

A job advert should have three main parts: a beginning, middle and conclusion with a call to action. Earlier in the book I mentioned the acronym AIDA, which stands for: attention, interest, desire and action. We'll be applying this to our job adverts.

The job title is the first thing that attracts the attention of candidates. It also contains keywords used by search engines to find the job advert. Therefore, ensure the job title is clear and relevant. If the role is for a Finance Director, put Finance Director and do not use abbreviations such as FD. The more accurate the job title is the more appropriate the applications will be.

The beginning, which is the opening paragraph, is what you use to capture the candidate's interest and entice them to read further. You should summarise the role by explaining what it is, what type of company it is, where it is and why they should read on.

If you read many job adverts they will usually open up by explaining what a *fantastic*, or *career advancing* opportunity it is and how *forward-thinking* the company is. These are powerful selling words to grasp the attention of the candidate, but in most cases there's no reason given as to why it's a *fantastic* opportunity. So they lose their impact. If you say it is a *dynamic role* you must follow it up with a reason why, otherwise such words will have little effect on the candidate and your job advert will fail to differentiate from the rest.

An example could be:

> *The Rich Recruiter is currently recruiting for a Commercial Accountant to join an energetic tech start-up, which has just opened in London's prestigious city centre. This is a career advancing opportunity as you will have the opportunity to create key financial processes from scratch, manage a team of five and help drive the business forward.*

As you'll see above, I appeal to candidates on multiple levels by selling the role, the company and the location. You may find that it is easiest to write the opening paragraph last, as you'll have a better feel for your job advert once you have written the body.

There is no set way to set out the body of your job advert, but it should include the following sections:

About the company - Tell the candidate what type of company it is, such as whether it's a retail company or a manufacturing company. Explain the size of the company, how long it has been established, any future plans, awards it has won and anything else that is factual and appealing. I always explain what the company culture is like whether it's fast paced, friendly or hardworking. Remember that you're trying to attract the perfect candidate. If someone works at a fast pace, but the company is laid back then there is a mismatch of cultures between the candidate and company. Somewhere along the process, this mismatch will come to light, and will cause you unnecessary problems and wasted time.

At the same time, while you must be informative you'll want to hold back some information from the job advert, because competing recruitment agencies may be able to interpret your job advert. Then they will contact and sell their own candidates to your client. To reduce the possibility of this happening you might write 'manufacturing' rather than 'food production', or write 'the London area' rather than a specific location.

The role and responsibilities – You'll need to inform the candidate about the duties and responsibilities of the role. Some recruitment consultants prefer to write these in paragraphs while some prefer to use bullet points. I always prefer bullet points as it allows candidates to scan the information more easily and match their skills to those in the bullet points.

One mistake recruitment consultants can make is to simply list the duties as is, for example:

• You will be required to analyse data

However, you must still put the duties in a more appealing way and continue to sell to the candidate. Analyse data, can therefore be transformed to:

• Analysis of data to identify key trends and help direct the company into profitable markets

While both bullet points advertise the same duty,

the second bullet point is more appealing. It explains what the candidate will actually be doing and how it plays an integral role in the growth of the company.

Additional information – In this section, write about any benefits that come with the role and the company, such as: training, pensions, childcare, flexible hours, free parking, a car, mobile telephone, laptop, holidays and anything else. I've always found that these are big motivators for candidates. It goes without saying, but do not make these up just to attract the perfect candidate.

They could pull out of the recruitment process once the truth comes out, leaving you in an undesirable situation.

Person specification – In this section, describe the skills, qualifications, personality, and attributes the ideal candidate would have. Explain what software systems they should be experienced in and what industry background they should ideally come from.

Call to action - The last section of the job advert is the call to action. This is an instruction to the candidates on how they can apply for the role. For example:

If you are an ideal fit for this vacancy, please do not hesitate to apply by clicking the apply button or emailing your CV to Andrew Leong at andrew@therichrecruiter.com.

Keywords

To ensure that your job advert is search engine friendly and easily found by your perfect candidate it must include keywords. Keywords are words that the candidate will use to search for the advertised role. The most important and relevant keywords will be those in the job title and these need to be used throughout the body of the job advert.

Polishing your Job Advert

It's important that your job advert is accurate. You're advertising both your personal brand and the recruitment company you work for. At the same time, your client will probably take the time to go online and review the job advert. You could receive a telephone call from your client if they're unhappy with the quality, or they believe you have mis-sold the vacancy. Ensure that you:

- Re-read the job advert
- Check the salary is correct
- Write in paragraphs
- Check spelling, grammar and punctuation
- Use bullet points when necessary

• Ensure your contact details are correct

Always get a colleague to check the job advert before you publish it.

Publishing your Job Advert

You must know your audience and where they'll look for vacancies. If you're recruiting for a senior position then you should post your job advert on jobs boards and websites that senior candidates use. Different jobs boards are targeted at different audiences and at different levels. While posting your job advert everywhere seems like a good marketing idea, it will lead to unnecessary work as irrelevant candidates will apply for the position.

Fake Job Adverts

As explained in an earlier section it's always easier to find candidates if you already have them on your candidate database. The reason for this is that job adverts take time to attract the right candidates. They can take hours, days or even weeks.

Therefore, to ensure your hot candidate list and your candidate database is always up-to-date you'll need to constantly post job adverts.

What if you don't have any vacancies to advertise? It's not uncommon for recruitment agencies to post fake job adverts. That is, post adverts for jobs that don't exist. They do this so that they're constantly building up a reserve of good candidates. They're being proactive rather than reactive. Now when a client calls up with a vacancy, it's likely that the agency will already have the perfect candidate on the candidate database. Before implementing such a strategy check with the laws in your area, check with the rules of the job boards you use, check with the rules of any associations and institutes your company is a member of and check with your manager. At the time of writing most recruitment agencies in the UK conduct such a practice.

Now recruitment consultants will usually be targeted to write job adverts, real or fake. However, they'll usually put minimal effort into the fake job adverts, because they're just trying to hit their target. Rich recruiters don't do this. They don't just post any job advert to hit a target. Rich recruiters treat fake job adverts the same as real ones, so that they attract the best candidates. They post job adverts based on their client's expected and predicted needs. That is, when writing an advert they write it with a specific client in mind. This'll ensure they have a ready supply of relevant candidates for their clients should a job be called in. At the same time, they can use these candidates to do speccing calls.

How do they manage candidates with a fake job advert, and is this right? When candidates send in their CV rich recruiters will follow up the candidates with a telephone interview. We'll discuss telephone interviews later in this book. After they've interviewed the candidate, they'll have a better understanding of their needs. Using this knowledge they put the candidate off the role. For example, they'll ask the candidate what their top three motivators are. If the candidate says: money, progression and a hard working environment. Rich recruiters might reply with:

> *"I don't think this job would suit you. The company has a five year pay freeze, and a notoriously slow and laid back environment. However, if you don't mind I would like to keep your details on file and contact you about any other suitable vacancies that arise."*

In this scenario, the rich recruiter has used the candidate's motivators to turn them off the job, and the candidate will be thankful for this rather than feel rejected.

Many readers will think this is morally wrong, disheartening and a waste of time for candidates who've applied for the role. I agree, it's controversial and I wish this was something that wasn't practiced in the industry. Unfortunately, it is practiced and it's highly likely your competitors will be doing such an activity, which means they'll always be bringing in a fresh supply of candidates. It goes without saying that when rich recruiters post a fake job advert they still treat candidates who apply with respect and courtesy. Recruitment consultants do have a difficult job and they're constantly chasing targets and money, but you don't have to lose sight of being a good person.

In summary, job adverts help to attract new candidates or make you aware of already existing candidates. Additionally, a constant presence of well-written job adverts is good marketing for your company and for your personal brand. Candidates, clients and competitors will keep seeing your name and your company brand on the adverts. As a result, candidates will find you; clients will call you and competitors will feel uneasy about your presence. Rich recruiters are knowledgeable about their market. They know what types of vacancies are hard to recruit for and what candidates a client may need in the future. They use fake job adverts to supply the candidate database for future trends. They see this as no different from supermarkets increasing their supply of BBQs before the summer period, or their antihistamine tablet supply before the hay fever season.

MATCHING A CANDIDATE TO A JOB

Matching a candidate to a job involves taking the job specification and matching the candidate's skills, experience, education and personality. The more the candidate matches the more likely the client will want to interview the candidate and hire them.

If a food production company wants to hire a Finance Director, who has industry experience, management experience, has professionally qualified through a big four finance firm and knows how to produce financial reports for shareholders. Then you find a Finance Director who has worked in the food production industry, who has management experience, who has qualified through a big four finance firm and has experience of producing financial reports for shareholders.

I've heard on numerous occasions from clients that recruitment consultants would send over CV's that didn't match the job specification, or they sent over their entire candidate database. This is ludicrous. From the client's perspective the whole point of using a recruitment consultant is to save time and prevent doing unnecessary work, so that they can carry on with their daily duties.

To ensure your client sees you as a top recruitment consultant, someone to come back to again, who saves them time and money, you should only send your client a handful of CV's from candidates you have interviewed and who match the job description.

What happens when you can't find the perfect candidate, or any candidates that match near to the job description? There'll be times when you can't find the right candidate due to a skill shortage, or the client not wanting to pay the right salary. As a recruitment consultant it's your job to consult the client. It's you that has the expert knowledge about the labour supply. Your client will respect you for consulting them, so rather than not sending them any CV's explain to them why you can't find a suitable candidate.

This leaves you several options to give to the client.

Firstly, you can ask your client to relax the job specification by asking them what could be overlooked. Secondly, you can ask them to increase the salary. If the client won't make any adjustments to the specification, offer to send them some CV's that may be more suitable alternatives. If the client is still reluctant it's best to tell the client that they should use an alternative recruitment agency. I know this is a difficult thing to do, but your client will appreciate your honesty and they'll come back to you in the future. Furthermore you don't have the time to work on vacancies that are costing you money, because every hour you're looking for that non-existent candidate, you're not selling or placing other jobs.

I broke onto my patch by working the vacancies that other agencies couldn't fill. However, even sometimes I was left in a position where the client's expectations were unrealistic. Assess each situation in detail and ask yourself if you're giving up too easily, or does it make better business sense to drop the vacancy.

TELEPHONE INTERVIEWS

When you find the right CV you'll need to call the candidate to give them an interview over the telephone.

If it's the first time you've spoken to the candidate you'll need to introduce yourself, state the reason you're calling and then ask them if they're free to speak. If they're free to speak explain to them that you'd like to go through their CV with them and then you'd like tell them more about the job.

You'll need to ask them lots of questions, some including:

Current Situation
- What's your current employment situation?
- Are you looking for a new role?
- Why are you looking for a new role?
- What's your currently salary?

- What's your ideal salary?
- What's the lowest salary you would work for?
- Do you have your own car?
- Where would you be willing to travel to?
- What's your notice period, and is it negotiable?

Achievements

- Tell me about a time when you exceeded your manager's expectations?
- Tell me about your proudest achievement in work?
- What challenging situations have you faced?
- What was your greatest disappointment, or setback to date?

Motivations

- What three things would excite you in a job?
- What makes you get out of bed in the morning and go to work?
- What motivates you in work?
- Describe a time when you felt that you were recognised by your manager for good work and how did it make you feel?
- How important is responsibility to your career?
- What motivates you to finish a difficult task?
- How important are promotions to you?

- Tell me about a time you were rejected and what did you do?
- What types of companies would you like to work for?
- What do you like in your current, or did you like in your last role?
- What don't you like in your current role, or didn't like in your last role?
- What are the reasons for leaving your last role?
- What are your three career motivators?

Relationship Skills

- Describe a conflict with a colleague and how you resolved it?
- Tell me about a time when you had to deal with a difficult customer and how you handled the situation?
- When was the last time you challenged senior management, and why?

Benefits

- What do think are your unique selling points?
- How do you feel you contribute to a company?
- What do you excel at?
- What are you main skill sets?

Competitors

- Are you with any other agencies?
- Which agencies are you with?
- How are you finding them?
- Have they got you any interviews? Where?

Leads

- Do you have any interviews coming up? Where?
- What roles have you recently applied for?
- What's the name of the person interviewing you?

Once you've captured the information from your candidate, give them the opportunity to ask you any questions. I personally wouldn't ask every question above, just those that are relevant.

Notice you should ask the candidate if they have any other interviews. This is another opportunity to identify clients who are recruiting.

At the end of the telephone interview you'll either want to discard the candidate, file them away for a different role or sell them the job and meet with them. If they're not suitable for the role tell them, but explain that you'll keep them on file should a more suitable position arise. If they're suitable this leads on to the next section.

INTERVIEWING CANDIDATES FACE-TO-FACE

A face-to-face interview is the next logical step from a telephone interview. Whether you conduct face-to-face interviews with candidates will largely depend on the type of candidates you recruit, the sector you recruit in and the company you work for. I know recruitment agencies that don't do interviews and I know recruitment agencies that won't put any candidate forward for any position unless they've been interviewed.

In general, if your candidates are local you should interview them in person. There are several reasons for interviewing candidates:

- They may be better in person than on paper
- They may be better on paper than in person
- They may have the right personality that fits

perfectly for the company you're recruiting for, which will not necessarily show on paper

- They may not have the right personality for the company you're recruiting for, which will not necessarily show on paper
- This is your opportunity to see how they interview and provide them with any feedback to improve their interview technique
- It helps to build a relationship with your candidate who will often become a client
- If they do become a client, even if you're not the recruitment agency that placed them, they'll see how professional and sharp you are
- Clients will feel they're getting their money's worth if you interview candidates

When inviting the candidate to meet with you get them to bring their qualifications and identifications for you to photocopy. Then save these for your records. I strongly suggest that you check they have any professional qualifications they claim. You don't want to sell a candidate only to be called by your client who's found out that your candidate lied about their qualifications.

Your interview should have a structured agenda, such as:

- Go through the candidate's CV and background
- Go through what they're looking for in their next role
- Tell them more about the company you work for
- Discuss the job they've applied for
- Give them the opportunity to ask any questions
- Discuss what happens next and close

You'll need to explain the agenda with the candidate in order for you to maintain control of the interview and establish the criteria.

For example:

"The structure of this meeting is to go through your CV, learn more about you, understand what you're looking for, tell you more about the <your company> and then tell you more about the job you've applied for. Then you'll have the opportunity to ask me any questions."

Many of the questions you ask in the interview may be the same as those that you asked on the telephone, so tell them that you may go over some of the same questions again.

A typical interview should last between 30 and 45 minutes. Stick to your agenda and don't let the conversation go off topic. At times you might need to tell the candidate they're not answering the question and ask if they could be more explicit with their answers. I've been in interviews where the candidate would talk endlessly about the company they've worked for rather than the role they did. In one interview, when I first began in recruitment, the candidate pulled out aerial maps of the company he worked for to show me which building he worked in. He then proceeded to tell me the operations of the company. While I enjoyed his enthusiasm it was irrelevant and it didn't add value to his application. Don't let the interview go off topic. Politely, but assertively direct the candidate back to the question. If the candidate is good and they're likely to be a client then I recommend spending a little more time than usual with them. If during the interview you identify that the candidate doesn't have the right skills and experience for any vacancy, then you may want to keep your interview shorter than 30 minutes. However, explain to the candidate that you're unable to help them and tell them why you can't.

It's likely that the candidate you're interviewing has worked for one of your clients or prospect clients. Use the interview to gather intelligence about your clients. This is extremely important to do especially if they've worked for a prospect client you're having trouble progressing with.

During the interview don't just assess the candidate's answers to the questions, assess everything. Did they turn up on time? Do they look you in the eye when speaking? Are they nervous? Are they wearing the right clothing for the industry? What's their body language like?

If at the end of the interview you feel they're a good candidate, but they're showing some weaknesses, help them identify them. For example if the candidate is late, or doesn't appear confident or dresses inappropriately, explain to them that you've picked this up and so will the client. Give them advice that they should arrive early, maintain strong eye contact and wear the correct clothing for the interview.

Most of the time, a good CV and a good telephone conversation will correlate with a good candidate in person. However, on occasions after you interview a candidate you'll get a gut feeling they're just not right. At this point you'll need to decide whether you want to submit their CV to the client or not. In other cases you'll definitely know not to progress with a particular candidate. Follow your gut feeling.

SELLING A ROLE TO A CANDIDATE

I n most sales positions you sell a service or product that doesn't have a mind of its own. It doesn't have an opinion, family commitments, work commitments, car breakdowns or any other obstacles that humans can bring. When selling products or services once you win a client you can, to a degree, deliver them with much more ease. If there are any issues, you can quickly resolve them with little disruption to the client's business. Recruitment is very different, and candidates are one of the most challenging aspects of recruitment. There is nothing worse than going through the whole recruitment process only to have your candidate pull out at the last minute and turn down your job offer. This is frustrating for the client and heart breaking for you.

However, this can be easily managed. My rule on this is: the less you have to persuade your candidate the easier the process will be. If your candidate is keen they're more than likely to show up to the interview and they're more than likely to accept the job. A common mistake is that you have to convince candidates to go to interviews and take jobs. While there is some sense and logic in persuading your candidates, it should be minimal. If you have to do a hard sell to the candidate it means they're not that keen. When a candidate isn't keen there's a high probability that they'll drop out at some stage in the process. This can cause you a great amount of stress, it'll probably irritate your client and you'll feel embarrassed. These feelings are only amplified if it's the first time you're recruiting for a client, especially one who's taken you many months, even years to win.

So the first thing to remember is that you shouldn't have to sell hard to convince your candidate to go to an interview. If they're not that interested, move past them and save your client and yourself the hassle.

To sell a role to a candidate you must first understand your candidate. You'll need to know: what excites them, what makes them get out of bed in the morning and where they want to go in their career. You'll have the answers to these questions from your telephone interview. See the chapter on telephone interviews.

Once you know these qualities about your candidate you can then sell them the role. Remember a sale is about matching wants and needs with a service or product. So if your candidate wants career progression and the vacancy has career progression then sell it to them. If the candidate wants a friendly laid back environment and the vacancy is for a friendly company then sell it to them. There's no point selling a dead end job to a candidate who wants progression, or to sell a progressive role to a candidate who wants to sit in a role for the next ten years.

PROTECTING YOUR VACANCY

Candidates are notorious for leaking your business intelligence to your competitors. I'm sure some candidates do this by accident and I'm also sure some do it on purpose. Either way you need to prevent information leaking about your vacancies.

When approaching candidates about a role, you'll face two situations: one, the candidate is on the database, or two, you've found their details elsewhere. In both cases you'll want to telephone interview and assess the candidates before you start to discuss the role with them. The reason for this is that it'll provide you with the information to sell to the candidate and it'll enable you to qualify them before giving them your top secret details about the vacancy.

So how do you approach a candidate about a vacancy and at the same time keep it secret? When approaching the candidate introduce the conversation in a way that allows you to keep control. One example could be the following:

"I'm currently recruiting for a position that I think you would be suitable for. Can we go through your details to see if it's a good fit for you?"

If the candidate agrees and asks you what the role is, avoid this question by telling them that you'll inform them about everything once you've gone through their details. This gives you the option to discard the candidate if they're not suitable while at the same time protecting the identity of your client.

If they're not suitable you can let them down gently and at the same time make them lose interest by telling them the job is the opposite of what they want. If they still ask for the name of your client, simply tell them that the client has asked you to keep it confidential at this point, and that you must honour your client's request. This'll keep your candidate happy and not provide them with any information to leak.

What if they're a good fit for the role? If at the end of the telephone interview you think they're a good fit for the role, this is when you would start to sell to your candidate. You should tell them the company name and tell them about the company. To sell the role to the candidate you should refer to the answers they gave to your interview questions.

You'll need to tell the candidate to keep this opportunity confidential. Some candidates will agree, but fail to understand why. If they fail to understand why then they're likely to discuss it with other recruitment agencies. It's essential you tell them and educate them exactly why they must keep it confidential. Inform them that if they tell another recruitment agency, that other recruitment agency will send CV's to the client making it even more competitive to get the job.

Unfortunately, you'll face situations where some of your competitors will send CV's of candidates to clients without asking the candidate's permission. Then once they get a buy in from the client they'll start selling the role to the candidate whose CV they sent. This can cause you problems if you've already spoken to that candidate first and they've given you permission to represent them. You can help to reduce this event by building strong relationships with your candidates and asking them to send you a representation email for that particular role, for example:

Hi <Your name>

This email is to confirm that I am being represented and only represented by <your company> for the role of <position> at <client's name>. I have not given permission to any other recruitment agency to represent me for this position, nor have I applied to this position directly.

Kind regards

<candidate's name>

If you wanted to make this more official and corporate looking you could create a word processed document with your company branding. Then print it off and have your candidate sign it. You may consider making this a company template for your business.

In this section we've looked at how to sell roles to candidates, which involves matching the candidate's motivations with the opportunities of the client. If they're not keen on the job quickly move on to another candidate rather than use a hard sell. You've also learnt how to reduce the possibility of candidates leaking your job to other recruitment agencies, as well as getting your candidates to provide you with a representation letter.

SELLING A CANDIDATE

When you're sure you've found the right candidate or candidates, it's time to sell the candidates to the client. This is slightly different from speccing a candidate, which we discussed earlier in the book, because the client is expecting you to deliver candidates. In this section I've split selling a candidate into three parts: preparing a CV, preparing a reference and selling the candidate to your client. For simplicity, I've used the word candidate to mean both 'a candidate' and 'several candidates', as the process is the same regardless.

PREPARING A CV

You'll need to prepare your candidate's CV for your client to review. Clients use CV's to assess the potential of candidates and decide if they want to interview them or not. Therefore, your candidate may or may not get an interview based on their

CV alone. For that reason, it's extremely important to be a good CV writer. A CV is like a shop window, and if it doesn't look appealing customers will walk away. The same applies to CV's. However, if you've done your recruitment correctly, preparing a CV becomes much simpler and you'll significantly increase the chances of securing an interview for your candidate.

So what does an appealing CV look like? There are three main points:

- Format
- Relevancy
- Language

Format

We'll skim through format, because the recruitment agency you work for should have a standard format, or a CV template to work from. If not please visit *www.therichrecrutier.com* for a CV template you can download and use. However, we'll briefly discuss why format is important. When we talk about format, I mean the layout of the CV with a consistent font throughout, the use of **bold** or *italics* for titles and the professional use of bullet points to break up paragraphs. The CV should also contain your recruitment agency's branding such as a logo and the company address.

Your client will be busy with their day job, so they'll want to be able to skim a CV and see all the key points including: qualifications, previous work experience, job titles and duties. Basically, this information needs to be presented, so the client doesn't need to search for it. They can just see it, instantly. If they can see what they're looking for in a few seconds, the more chance they'll want to interview your candidate. They'll also hold you more favourably, as you've made the job easier for them.

Relevancy

The next point is 'relevancy' and if you can master this skill, you'll drastically increase the number of interviews you get for your candidates. Using the job specification you took from the client, you may have found your candidate by matching the job specification to their CV. On the CV you submit to your client you must make that information more obvious to the client. You do this by rearranging the candidate's duties under their job titles so that the key points are at the very top. You can also reword job titles to suit your client's needs. Now you must not change the integrity of the CV, for example if they're an accountant you cannot change their job title to HR director. However, if they're an accountant who's done a lot of financial analysis in their role, you could change their job title to 'financial analyst', if that's what your client is looking for. The reason for this is that job titles can be ambiguous and one job title may not mean the same in another company. Make sure you've informed the candidate you've done this.

Language

The last point is 'language' and we can break this down further into:

- Power words
- Informative language
- Numbers (quantifiable achievements)

Power words are words that go at the beginning of a bullet point under the candidate's duties. They help to sell your candidate by changing a basic duty into a dynamic one, for example:

"Exceeded sales targets", becomes "Successfully exceeded sales targets."

In addition to using power words the language you use should be positive and informative, for example:

"Successfully exceeded sales targets", becomes "Successfully exceeded sales targets on a daily basis."

Numbers and quantifiable achievements also help

to sell the candidate as it enables the client to measure the information they've been given. Don't put a number or a percentage on every bullet point, this would be too much information for the client to absorb. However, if used sparingly numbers have a great impact, for example:

"Successfully exceeded sales targets on a daily basis", becomes "Successfully exceeded sales targets by 20% on a daily basis".

Reviewing the original duty "Exceeded sales targets", it has now evolved into "Exceeded sales targets by 20% on a daily basis". This is a lot more informative and appealing to read than the original duty. It shows the candidate in a more attractive light, which can mean the difference between getting an interview or not.

Many recruitment agencies, especially if you work for a larger recruitment agency, have recruitment resourcers to write and format CV's. Use a resourcer smartly so that they save you time, but don't become dependent on them. While they're a benefit, you should get into the routine of writing CV's yourself. As explained earlier you can't rely on a resourcer all the time. You can write and format CV's outside of core hours to prevent it cutting into your sales time.

In all cases, once you've changed the candidate's CV into your required format, send the CV to the candidate along with the job specification and tell them to add to the CV any duties, numbers and achievements that match the specification. Once they send it back to you, you can then add your professional touch by rewording it to make it more appealing.

Getting the candidate to alter and upgrade their CV has another purpose. It also enables you to assess how compliant and how keen they are for the role. If they don't help you fix up their own CV then you know they're not that keen for the role. If they're not that keen for the role it will probably cause you problems later on in the process.

CV writing, like any skill, gets easier and better the more you do it. As you write and send out CV's you'll see what works and what doesn't. Try to constantly criticise the CV and question yourself regarding why a client has responded and why they haven't responded. You'll soon get to a stage that once you write and format a CV you know it will be well received by the client.

When a client does get back to you about a CV, it's important to ask the client:

- What they liked about the CV

• What they didn't like about the CV

They might say they liked the candidate's education or they liked that the candidate had worked for a multinational company. Whatever the client says, record this information on your client database and use it to sell. If the client says they liked the candidate's voluntary work, advise your candidate to talk about it in the interview. Additionally, you can also use this information to do speccing calls in the future.

PREPARING A REFERENCE

References are a great way to help you sell your candidate, especially in a situation where your client cannot decide between two candidates. A strong reference can help sway their decision in your favour. The recruitment agency you work for will probably have a standard reference sheet, and there should be a facility to electronically file it away for the candidate for any future vacancies. If not you can download one from *www.therichrecrtuier.com*.

When you're putting a candidate forward for a job and if you're getting their reference for the first time, always tailor the reference to that job. I don't mean alter it to suit your purposes. I mean get their referee to tailor it by asking them to focus on certain criteria, which you know your client is looking for.

How do you get the referee to tailor the reference for you? Firstly, when taking the job specification from the client, you should ask questions along the lines of:

- "What are the three main things you are looking for in a candidate?"
- "What three things are most important in your ideal candidate?"

For demonstration purposes let's say the client responds: "Confidence, ability to deal with clients and a team player."

Now when you take the reference you can guide the referee by asking them to comment on the candidate's confidence, ability to deal with clients and their teamwork skills.

In some cases, when the referee has a good relationship with the candidate. You can send the referee a blank reference sheet and ask them to write about the candidate's confidence levels, ability to deal with clients and their team work skills. Advise the referee that if they write about how good the candidate is in these areas, the candidate will more than likely get the job. Usually, the referee will be more than willing to help, as they'll want to see their old work colleague get the job.

Ideally, you'll want to get and send the candidate's reference with their CV. If you've had to send the CV first, then send the reference as soon as possible. Always try to get a reference for your candidate. It's such a powerful tool to use and can often swing a decision in your favour.

What happens if you can't get a reference? There'll be times when you can't get a reference. Maybe the candidate is still in their first job and then obviously you can't approach their current employer for one. Maybe the candidate is new to the country or their previous manager has moved country. In these cases, you can always use their LinkedIn testimonials as references. If the candidate doesn't have any LinkedIn testimonials ask the candidate to get one or two.

What happens if the candidate receives a bad reference? There'll also be times that your candidate receives a bad reference. This can range from just a bland or poor reference to a severely bad one. Ones I've heard in the office have ranged from stealing money to fraud.

It's always best to supply a good reference to support your candidate's application, and clients will think they're getting their money's worth if you're seen to be going that extra mile. However, if their reference is just bland or poor then generally I would dismiss it and not submit it to the client. Only do this if you have met the candidate and they "feel" good to you. I've met brilliant candidates, but they received a poor or bland reference from a bad or jealous manager. The important thing was that I met the candidate in person and I made this judgement myself.

If you meet a candidate and you get a bad gut feeling about them, but you also take a bad reference, then you may want to consider pulling your candidate, or at least discussing this with your client and asking them for their thoughts. This sounds counterproductive, but it'll save you and your client time and money. If you don't consult your client and they accept your candidate, but they turn out to be disruptive in a negative way then you'll get the blame.

You may meet a candidate who's brilliant in person, but they receive a reference about illegal activity or fraud. Depending where you recruit it could be a legal requirement for you to inform your client, at the very least you should do this for ethical reasons. Firstly, check with the candidate before you do tell the client to gain their permission. Also check with your management to ensure you're up-to-date with current employment laws

SELLING A CANDIDATE TO THE CLIENT

Sending a formatted and tailored CV with a reference is only part of the job. You'll also need to send a sales email which has the CV attached. You'll then need to follow this up with a telephone call.

The aim of the email is to create some interest and excitement for the client, which will make them want to read the CV. You'll need to keep the email short and snappy, as the client won't want to read all the candidate's skills in an email and then read them again on the CV. Just give them enough information to spark that interest. To do this, follow the power of three using three key points to hook your client. The three key points should be what your client is looking for the most, which you'll have identified in the job specification and various conversations with them.

The email should have a beginning, middle and an end, which looks like:

- An Introduction
- A sell
- A guide to the next stage

For example:

Hi Alison,

Please see attached the CV and reference of **Steven Jones,** *in summary:*

- *5 years in a food production company*
- *1ˢᵗ class degree in Finance from a red brick university*
- *Management experience leading a team of 12*

I will call you this afternoon to talk you through Steven's details.

Kind regards,

Andrew Leong

The last part of the email with reference to calling the client has many purposes. Firstly, it informs the client you're calling. Secondly, it creates a powerful professional image and shows that you're taking charge of the situation. Thirdly, again clients will think they're getting their money's worth with a professional touch rather than a recruitment consultant just forwarding them CV's. Lastly, you'll want to verbally sell your candidate too. The client might have reservations about the CV, so you'll need to resolve these. Your aim at this point is to secure an interview for your candidate. If the client doesn't like the CV you'll be able to ask why and then either convince them otherwise, or using this information, go back to the labour market for another candidate.

There'll be times when the client cannot see the link between what they want and the CV you've provided to them, even though you've made the key points obvious. In this case you'll need to highlight this to the client. You can do this gently by saying something, such as:

"You might have missed this on the candidate's CV, but if you look on page one of the CV you'll notice they've experience in..."

There have been times when a client has asked me for candidates with specifics and I've provided them with CV's containing those specifics. Only for the client to tell me the candidates didn't fit with what they wanted. In this case I absolutely knew I had delivered and I had to challenge the client. This type of conversation may go as follows:

"I'm confused, have you read the CV? You've asked for..., and I've given you... I'm not sure what's missing?"

This may sound confrontational, but you'll at times face clients who you need to stand your ground with. If you don't they won't respect you. This is rare though, and most will be fine if you gently point them in the right direction.

As mentioned earlier, whether the client wants to interview your candidate or not you should always ask these two questions:

- What did you like on their CV?
- What didn't you like on their CV?

This provides you with more intelligence on the client's needs and desires. From their feedback you may realise that you have a better candidate, so you'll want to send their details too.

In some cases, when you phone the client they'll have not looked at the CV. If the client has time, ask them to open up the CV and talk them through it. Then guide the client through the key points. The key points are the points that attracted you to the candidate and what the client is looking for in an employee. You can also discuss the candidate's fantastic personality you saw from the interview you did with them, which is something that wouldn't necessarily show through a CV.

Clients will ask you questions about the candidate and sometimes these questions will be unexpected, such as "Why did they pick those A levels," or "Why did they chose that university?" While it's important to know your candidates, it's near impossible to know enough to be able to answer all of the client's unexpected questions. In such a case be truthful with the client and say you don't know the answer, but you'll find out for them.

In this section we've looked at how to prepare and transform a candidate's CV into a winning one. We then looked at how to acquire a relevant reference for your candidate. We then looked at how to email your client in such a way that they'll read the CV you've sent them. This was followed with telephoning your client to discuss your candidate and securing them an interview.

INTERVIEW PREP

When your client informs you that they'd like to interview your candidate, you'll need to obtain as much information about the interview process as possible. To do this, ask your client questions along the following:

- When is the interview?
- Where is the interview being held?
- Who will be in the interview?
- Who will lead the interview?
- How long will the interview be?
- What does the candidate need to bring?
- What questions will be asked?
- What's the format of the interview?
- Who else are you interviewing?
- How many are you interviewing?
- Are the other candidates through a recruitment agency?
- Are any of the candidates internal employees?

- On paper, who's your favourite candidate?
- Will they be doing any tests?
- What type of tests?
- What will be on the tests?
- How will the tests affect the hiring decision?
- How many interview stages will there be?

Some clients will be more giving than others, but usually clients will give you this information. Asking these questions can feel awkward on your first time, but clients expect it and they understand that you need to prepare your candidate for the interview. If you don't ask your competitors will, which will mean they'll have better prepared candidates. This would reduce your chances of winning, so ensure you get as much detail about the interview format as possible to increase your chances.

Once you have the format of the interview you can now prepare your candidate and tell them what to reply to interview questions, what to wear, where to go and what time. Have this discussion on the telephone or in person, but also send it to them via email, so they have it written down. In the same email, attach the candidate's CV you sent to the client and get them to take a copy to the interview. Also attach any maps the client has provided along with detailed directions. Even encourage the candidate to do a practice commute to the interview so they know exactly where to go. This may seem over the top, but I've had candidates call me on the day of the interview asking me for directions and asking me to inform the client they'll be late, because they've got lost. You don't want this happening. Even if your candidate has an MBA and a PhD, provide them with every bit of detail about directions.

When you first speak with your candidate you'll want to ask them when they last interviewed and how they feel about interviews. Your candidate may have been in their role for many years and have forgotten how to interview. Go over body language and eye contact with them. It should be no different from the body language you would use in a sales meeting with your client, which was demonstrated earlier in this book.

Explain to your candidate that if the interviewer asks a question that they don't understand, it's important that they don't answer it. Instead, they should ask the interviewer to repeat the question or rephrase it. Assure them that not understanding a question and having the confidence to ask the interviewer to rephrase it is seen as positive.

Teach your candidates the STAR approach to answering questions, which stands for: situation, task, action and result. This is an extremely powerful way to answer interview questions. When I began teaching my candidates this technique their success rate significantly increased, which meant my placement rate increased.

It enables the candidate to answer a question in a structured manner, which makes the interviewer more receptive to the message.

I will explain the STAR approach in greater detail, but I'll explain it to you as if you're the candidate. If the interviewer asks you the question: "Can you describe a project you were involved in and what your role was?" You would at first explain the 'situation' or 'task' and describe what the project was about, how you got involved and what you were trying to achieve.

The next part of your answer would be to demonstrate the 'action' you took and what you did. Ensure that you speak about yourself and what you did, not what 'we' or the 'team' did. Be detailed in your answer by explaining what you did, how you did it and why you did it. For example: "I was given the unexpected news that the project was being cut short, which meant we were behind schedule. Not wanting the project to fail I pulled everyone together to deliver the news and collect their thoughts. As expected they were disheartened, so

I reminded them how great it would be not only if we finished the project, but finished it in this new shorter timescale. I facilitated a problem solving session and we came up with a solution to finish the project on this new, more difficult date." Highlighting the reasons behind your actions in this way has a greater impact on the interviewer and it helps them understand your logic. It also reinforces the feeling that you're considering the consequences of your actions while also maintaining control.

The next stage of your answer is the 'result', which is when you explain what you achieved and what you learnt. For example: "As a result, we achieved the new, more difficult deadline date and we did it under budget saving £40,000. I learnt that by pulling the team together and enabling them to come up with the solution meant they had ownership of the project. This is what motivated them to get the project complete." This part of the answer is important, because it demonstrates that you achieved your goal, but you also step back to reflect and learn from your work.

I strongly recommend that you get familiar with the STAR approach and teach it to your candidates.

There is one question that candidates fear which is: "What's your biggest weakness." This is when most candidates use a stock answer such as "I'm a perfectionist." Instead encourage your candidate to reflect on a real weakness and an action they've taken to overcome it. They could do this using the star approach. A quick example: "I was asked to give a speech to the whole company for our annual conference about our successful project. I realised as I was giving the speech to 500 people that I was extremely nervous and it was not to the best of my ability. The very next day I booked myself onto public speaking courses and I've dramatically improved." This shows the interviewer that your candidate is always trying to improve and they're aware of their own ability.

Teach your candidate to ask lots of questions at the interview. Questions demonstrate to the interviewer that the candidate is interested in the company. Insightful questions also demonstrate intelligence. Remember that asking questions is fundamental to selling, and candidates are selling themselves at the interview. Examples of questions can include:

- What's the culture of the department like?
- What projects are running at the moment?
- What projects are planned for the future?
- What obstacles do the company / department currently face?

- As an employee how could I exceed your expectations?
- What's the reason for the vacancy?
- What's the career progression potential at your business? (Don't ask if the client wants the candidate to sit in the same role for many years)
- What's your management style like?
- How do you plan to deal with changes in the market?
- How can I help the company meet its goals?
- What are the company's strengths and weaknesses?

A powerful question that you should get your candidates to ask near the end of the interview is:

- Do you have any reservations about me?

Clients might have doubts about the candidate, so this gives your candidate the opportunity to convince the client otherwise.

If you recruit for sales professionals then your client will be testing your candidate's ability to close a sale, so a good question to demonstrate this ability is to get your candidate to ask the question:

- Can I have the job?

The client will like the fact that your candidate has tried to close the job. This works very well when interviewing for recruitment positions, so if you're a recruitment-to-recruitment consultant, ensure your candidate closes like this. If you have multiple candidates going to the interview don't tell them all to ask the same questions. This will make them look too prepared by you and the creditability of their questions will be drastically reduced.

Ask your candidate what they plan on wearing to the interview and guide them to the appropriate clothing. Also remind them to take notes during the interview.

It's important that you teach your candidate not to do or say certain things in the interview, including:

- Put their elbows on the interviewer's desk
- Read any of the interviewers documents on the desk
- Argue, get angry or emotional
- Negotiate or discuss salary
- Talk badly about any previous employee or employer
- Unprofessional behaviour such as talking about sex
- Say anything derogatory
- Eating food or chewing gum

- Slouch
- Yawn
- Be distracted by anything in or outside the room
- Bite nails or hide behind their hands
- Use any electronic devices such as a mobile telephone

As well as prepping the candidate you'll also need to prep the client. Sometimes clients forget that it's a two way road. They expect that if a candidate is interviewing that they automatically want the job. This can especially happen if it's a big brand. You'll need to remind them that they'll also have to sell the company to the candidate.

If you have multiple candidates going to the interview, you'll probably favour one candidate as your strongest. In this case, you'll want to arrange interviews so that your favourite candidate interviews last. The reason for this is so that you can gather information about the interview process from your other candidates and then pass this information on to your strongest candidate. This leads us on to the next section about debriefing candidates after their interview.

CANDIDATE INTERVIEW
FEEDBACK

After the interview, you'll need to speak to your candidate and the client to get their feedback. Ensure that you speak to your candidate first and not the client first, you'll see why later. When you've phoned your candidate ask them questions such as:

- How did the interview go?
- Do you think you did well?
- How long where you in there for?
- What did they ask you?
- Was the interview the same as what I told you?
- Where there any surprises?
- Did they say when a decision will be made?
- Did you like the company?
- Can you see yourself working there?

- What do you think of the interviewer?
- Are there any areas you felt weak on which you would like me to bring up with the client?
- Were there any areas that you felt you could've covered better, or that you don't feel you were able to express your skills and abilities in the best light?
- Do you think they have any reservations about you?
- How do you feel about the job now you've interviewed?
- If they offered you the job would you take it?

Questions such as these allow you to make judgements of whether your candidate did a good interview, or not. For example, if the client said interviews would be around 60 minutes and your candidate says they were only interviewed for 20 minutes, you may question whether it was a successful interview. If your candidate was in for longer than 60 minutes, usually this is a positive sign.

Ask your candidate if they think the client might have any reservations about them and what they'd be. Ask them if they think they didn't answer a particular question well and what they should have said instead. Record their new ideal answer and prepare to bring this up with the client.

Once you have the candidate's feedback, you can now call the client and ask how the interview went.

If it's a one interview process and your client liked your candidate, then they'll usually respond by saying they'd like to employ the candidate. We'll discuss what to do when your client wants to employ your candidate in the next section.

Sometimes, the client will have reservations about your candidate and this is why you need to speak to the candidate first. In such a case, you'll need to ask lots of questions to ascertain why your client has reservations.

Once you understand why, you can use your candidate's feedback to counter the reservations. For instance, if the client says the candidate didn't answer a particular question well, you can now respond to the client by saying that the candidate understood this. Now you can tell the client what the candidate really wanted to say. If the client is still unsure, ask if they'd like to meet the candidate again.

Try hard for your candidate, especially if you truly believe they'll benefit the client's company. In this case, the client will hear the passion and genuineness in your voice and may agree for an additional interview. Whatever you do, do not force your candidate upon your client to hit commission or targets. No one likes a pushy sales person. The client is making a big decision, so they want your support and trust. If they don't want your candidate and you actually agree with their reasons, support their decision. Show your client that you fully understand why, but now you have a better understanding of what they want you can recommend another candidate or go back to the market. They'll appreciate that more.

MAKING AN OFFER TO THE CANDIDATE

When your client wants to hire your candidate it's truly an exciting time, but you'll need to keep calm and stay professional. Remember to keep asking questions:

- What did you like about them?
- What where their strengths?
- When do you want them to start?
- Can I reconfirm the salary with you?
- Are there any changes to the role?

When you feel you have all the information from the client you can go back to the candidate and offer them the role. This is a fantastic part of the job and it's a beautiful feeling hearing or seeing the candidate get excited by the offer.

Candidates can become scared by the prospect of

leaving their secure job for another job, so keep reassuring them. Relate the new job back to their three career motivators we discussed earlier.

Ask the candidate when they plan to hand in their notice. This is a potential barrier to your sales as their current employer may make them a counter offer. Consult your candidate and inform them that their current employer may make them a counter offer. As you can see, your deal isn't 100 percent closed yet and you don't want your candidate to drop out last minute. Ask your candidate what they'd do if their employer made them a counter offer.

Explain to your candidate that if their current employer valued them, they wouldn't wait for them to hand in their notice before offering them a pay rise. Emphasise that if they did take the pay rise and stayed with their existing employer, their employer would always question their loyalty.

Once your candidate has told you when they plan to hand in their notice, mark it in your diary to call them afterwards. When you speak to your candidate they'll usually say everything is fine and that they're still keen for the new role. In this case you can go back to the client and inform them that the candidate has handed in their notice. This is to reassure the client. Remember that this is also an exciting and happy time for the client, so share their excitement.

This is recruitment and not everything runs smoothly. Sometimes, candidates can be persuaded to stay by their current employer through such incentives as a higher salary. In this case you'll need to ask the candidate if you could get them an even higher salary would they still want to stay. If the candidate says that they'd still stay with their existing employer, ask them what they'd need to make the move into the new role. If they're unwilling to move wish them luck and inform your client what has happened. Be prepared to go back to the market and supply more CV's. If your candidate says they'd still be interested in the new role if you could increase their salary then this takes us into the next section, negotiating salaries.

NEGOTIATING THE SALARY

I n all cases you should record the salary the client is prepared to pay when you take down the job specification. You'll need to double check the salary and ask if they're flexible with it. If they're flexible ask what the boundaries are. The salary is important because it'll attract a particular calibre of candidate and it's what they expect to be paid.

However, you may face situations when the client tries to negotiate the salary down once they've chosen your candidate. Alternately your candidate may have been counter-offered and ask for a higher salary.

In this section we'll discuss both situations. If a client tries to negotiate the salary down try and convince them that this is a bad idea. It's a bad idea, especially for your fee rate, which is likely to be on a percentage. At the same time it'll make the candidate feel less worthy. Explain to the client that if they lower the salary from what was advertised they may lose the candidate. Inform them that even if the candidate does accept this lower salary they'll feel less valued and will be de-motivated before they even start the job.

If the client is still insistent on lowering the salary, explain to them that they have to bring something else to the table to balance the loss, such as: a salary review in six months, bonus opportunities, free parking, extra holidays, flexible hours, subsidised lunches or something else. You'll need something to go back to the candidate to cushion the impact of the reduced salary.

The client may or may not give you this, but when you go back to the candidate be open and honest. Inform them that they've been offered the job, but the client wants to reduce the salary, yet you have gotten them free parking or whatever you have managed to negotiate. The candidate might accept this in which case you would inform the client and the deal would be near to closure.

In the situation were the candidate says they do not accept the salary, ask them what salary would work for them. Then go back to the client and explain that the candidate refuses the salary drop and they'll not go lower than the salary originally offered. You may have to go back and forth between the client and the candidate a number of times. This type of negotiation can be one of the most enjoyable parts of recruitment. If clients and candidates are at loggerheads ask them to meet in the middle, for example the salary may have been advertised at £45,000 but the client now wants to pay £40,000. If neither will budge ask them both to meet in the middle at £42,500. The client will feel like they've won, because they've saved £2500. The candidate will feel like they've won, because they've increased a reduced salary by 2500. You'll have also won because you made the placement happen.

In the situation where the candidate wants more salary ask them what's changed on their end to prompt the increase. They may have been counter offered, or offered another job and now they're in a position to negotiate a higher salary. They may just be very confident and feel they're worth more.

In this situation you would call the client and explain the circumstances, for example the candidate has been offered another job. Clarify that the candidate is still interested, but that they'd like a higher salary. Then advise that if they don't want to lose the candidate they should increase the salary or match the offer made by the other company.

Remember, once you present this to the client stop talking even if the silence is long and awkward. If the client says "no", ask them if they can offer anything else, such as: bonus opportunities, free parking or more holidays. This situation could mirror the above where you're constantly going back and forth between the candidate and the client. Keep guiding the candidate and the client to meet halfway by asking the candidate to lower their expectations and the client to increase their offerings.

All clients and candidates are different, so assess each situation independently. Remember to keep negotiating. Get the client who comes in low to go higher with money or through other offerings, and get the candidate whose expectations are too high to come down and meet the client's offering.

In certain circumstances you may not want the candidate to lower their offer if you think they're worth it. Remember, a higher salary would mean a higher fee if you're working to a percentage of the salary.

It's unlikely that you'll lose a placement when negotiating a salary unless the candidate or client is being unreasonable. However, the fear of losing a placement, especially if your desk is struggling, can cripple your ability to negotiate. When you have this type of fear you can become too timid and you can end up begging the candidate to take the job. Never do this. Always be cool, calm and negotiate. Just remember there are plenty of opportunities out there. Sometimes it's powerful to say to the client or candidate "Take it or leave it."

AFTER SALES

Congratulations, you've made a placement, well done. Once your client has made the offer and your candidate has accepted the job you'll still need to provide them with excellent customer service.

Your candidate may be on a notice period, so keep in touch with them to see how they're doing. They'll appreciate the call. If you don't they may develop cold feet, or believe the opportunity has gone.

Once the candidate has started the job, call them and ask them how they're getting on. Ask them if they're happy. Remember candidates can still pull out from a job once they've started. No doubt your terms of business will have a refund period, also known as a rebate period, so you'll want to ensure your candidate stays put. That is unless they're having an absolutely miserable time in their new role.

Then you may want to consider a backup plan. If the candidate is unhappy, but you feel it's just a bit of a culture shock, encourage your candidate to stick through it and explain that things will get better once they've adjusted. As well as being an expert sales professional, headhunter, negotiator, career advisor and writer you'll also have to become an expert counsellor.

Also call the client and gain their feedback. Ask the client if they're happy and whether the candidate is doing a good job. One of the best compliments you can give someone is a complement from another person. If the client says the candidate is doing a good job tell the candidate. If the candidate has said the client is a good manger, tell the manager. You'll forge their relationship, secure your placement and build stronger relationships with both.

How To Write A Winning E-Shot

An e-shot is an email marketing message that is sent to a group of clients. It's a direct marketing approach because the email reaches your clients' email inbox. It's also known as email marketing.

These types of emails are not personal because they're sent on a mass scale. If you've ever bought goods from a website you'll probably receive similar marketing e-shots about deals and updates from that company. In recruitment you also send out e-shots about your products, which happen to be your candidates.

There are several reasons why I'm in favour of good e-shots:

- They enable you to market your products on a mass scale
- They help clients remember you and your brand
- They help to show your intelligence as a recruiter
- They can reach clients who won't take your telephone call
- Clients within a company will forward e-shots to each other
- They can bring in a large amount of out of office emails which hold mass amounts of information
- They pull in jobs

There's no doubt that if a client is recruiting and they receive a relevant e-shot they'll get in touch with you. In this section I'll show you how to write a winning e-shot and who exactly to send it to.

E-shots can be difficult to write when you first start producing them. It could take many e-shots before you find a winning formula that your particular clients respond to. However, the following tips will shorten your learning curve.

The first rule is to send the right e-shots to the right sectors and industries. Sending out a general e-shot to every client on your database will cause your reputation to decrease. As a result, your clients will either stop reading your emails, or they'll block your emails. If this happens you'll be missing a very important sales tool, so e-shots must be sector, industry and management level specific.

To begin with you'll need to identify what sector you want to send the e-shot to. You can do this in two ways: the first way is to find a good candidate and focus your e-shot around their industry experience. For example, if the majority of the candidate's work experience has been in the retail industry, you would send the e-shot to your retail clients. The second way is to find a candidate around an industry you want to specifically target. For example, if you want to send the e-shot to food production companies, you'll need to find a good candidate who has a history of working in food production.

Which method is best? I would use the first method every time I came across a strong candidate. I would use the second method when I wanted to target a specific sector. For example, you identify that the economy is having a property boom through reading newspapers, speaking to candidates and taking a couple of enquires from construction companies. Therefore, you have reason to believe construction companies and property management companies are going to be recruiting. I would then spend some time focusing on finding a good construction candidate to e-shot to my construction clients, and a property candidate to e-shot to my property management clients.

E-shots not only need to be tailored to a specific sector audience, but they need to be targeted to the right management level. Don't send a director of a large organisation an e-shot of a junior candidate, or send a junior manager an e-shot of a director level candidate. From the information you've gathered through telephone calls and research you'll have identified what management levels recruit what type of staff. Tag your client database with this information to ensure e-shots are targeted at the right management level.

Once you've selected your candidate to e-shot you'll then need to create the e-shot using the information from their CV. Many Recruitment Consultants will simply just copy and paste from a candidate's CV and consider it complete. This isn't an e-shot, but a CV in email form. While you'll need to copy elements of your candidate's CV, a winning e-shot has a specific layout, and is written in specifically chosen words. These words are not only persuasive sales words, but sector-specific words as each sector has their own language and abbreviations. Doing an e-shot this way is not only more visually and professionally appealing, but it causes your client to react in three ways: one, if they're recruiting they'll contact you back; two, if they're not recruiting they'll save your e-shots and continue to read any that you send in the future; three, they'll associate you as an intelligent recruitment consultant.

We've touched on the acronym AIDA a couple of times, but to remind you, it stands for: attention, interest, desire and action. You'll also need to apply this principle to your e-shots.

The structure of your e-shot should be as follows:

- Subject
- Introduction
- Body
  - Sector
  - Qualifications
  - Achievements
  - Experience
  - Testimonial / Reference (if possible)
- Call to Action
- Opt-out

I've created an example e-shot from the structure above. In this example I've used a financial analyst whose specific sector is retail.

Example E-shot

Subject: Qualified Retail Financial Analyst – Immediately Available

The Rich Recruiter is currently representing a highly experienced and qualified Financial Analyst. Candidate 123 specialises in building complex Excel spreadsheets for budgeting, planning and reporting models. Candidate 123 thrives in highly pressured and quick-delivery situations where they are known for delivering beyond expectations.

Sector: Retail

Qualifications: 1st class degree in Mathematics and CIMA qualified

Availability: Immediately

Systems: SAP, Oracle and advanced Excel modelling

Achievements

- Successfully saved £1m by implementing financial models
- Significantly increased sales by £500K through identifying market trends

Experience

Feb 2013 – Feb 2014 Retail Company

Position: Commercial Analyst

- Accurate commercial reporting and forecasts for Buying & Merchandising in advance of large shareholder refinancing
- Created Business Objects to produce a suite of reports analysing sales, promotions and stock
- Successfully created informative dashboards to summarise weekly performance
- Produced complex models to report on and forecast the sale of older, less-desirable stock

"Candidate 123 was a real asset to the company. Through their financial modelling we could predict future trends, which saved thousands."
– Finance Director

If you would like to discuss this candidate's details please do not hesitate to contact Andrew Leong on <telephone number> or via email at andrew@the-richrecruiter.com.

To stop receiving emails like this please email "stop" to andrew@therichrecruiter.com.

Your client will probably receive a large amount of marketing emails from all kinds of companies selling packaging, insurance and stationery, to name a few. Not to mention they'll also be receiving large amounts of e-shots from your competing recruitment companies. For these reasons, your e-shots have to be compact, easy-to-read, relevant and with key information that's effortless to find.

I make the subject of the e-shot as a clear as possible, so the client can see, instantly, exactly what I'm selling. In this case: a qualified retail financial analyst who's immediately available. The subject is enough to make the client want to read even if they aren't recruiting. However, should the client be busy and they're not recruiting then they can delete the email without hassle. You don't want your clients reading your e-shots at the expense of irritating them, so never use misleading subject titles. Imagine your client isn't recruiting and is having a bad day. You put a misleading e-shot subject title that causes them to read the e-shot wasting their time. You'll probably receive a nasty reply and have all future e-shots blocked, so it's better that to be clear and transparent. Remember, you're in this for the long run and eventually you'll send an e-shot at the right time resulting in you picking up a job.

I make the e-shot compact and easy to read using

bold subtitles. I then put all the important information at the top. When the client opens the e-shot they can see all the important information on their screen without needing to scroll down. They can make a very quick observation regarding whether the candidate is relevant or not. Subconsciously the client will favour this layout and welcome any future e-shots from you. Notice how I've put achievements above experience, because achievements can be 'benefits' to a client. Everyone has duties under work experience, but achievements suggest the candidate can bring something extra to the company. When interviewing a candidate I always ask them to tell me what they've achieved, so I can turn these into potential benefits for my clients.

I take all the content for my e-shot from the candidate's CV and tailor it to make it sound more persuasive. I do this by using power words, which we discussed earlier, for example: "created dashboards" becomes "successfully created informative dashboards".

If possible I put a testimonial or reference on the e-shot. A classic sales technique used by companies is to get customers to talk positively about their products and services. Consumers are more likely to buy in to and believe the review of another customer than the words of a sales professional. Some e-commerce companies do this brilliantly with their product reviews. Whenever customers go to purchase a product they check the customer reviews section to help them make a decision. The same principle applies to recruitment sales, so when possible I put a testimonial or reference to back up my e-shot.

In the next section I put a "call to action", with my name, telephone number and email address. This helps guide the client through the buying process by explaining what to do next.

In the last paragraph I explain what they need to do if they no longer want to receive e-shots. This is a legal requirement depending on what country you're from, but it also shows professionalism.

You'll notice that I put the candidate's reference number rather than their name. This is for several reasons. You don't want your client trying to find your candidate using websites such as LinkedIn where they can approach the candidate directly. You also need to protect the identity of the candidate. If your candidate is currently in a full time job, ensure your e-shot doesn't go to the company the candidate is working for. Also ensure your e-shot doesn't go to any of the candidate's previous employers or places of work. You may want to consider taking off any company names and replacing them with titles such as 'Retail Company' to help protect your candidate's identify.

How often should you send an e-shot? When a client receives too much email from the same person or company, it's called "spam". The client will simply click a button and block all future emails from you if you spam them with e-shots. That's if their spam filters don't do it first. The phrase "less is more" is relevant here and I would recommend sending an e-shot to each client about once per month. However, I recommend sending e-shots at least once a week. Tailor your e-shots and send them to specific sectors and specific managers. That way you're constantly sending e-shots out without sending them to the same person in the company every week. Tailored marketing always works best.

The worst time to send an e-shot is Friday afternoon. This is often done by recruitment consultants who are just looking to hit their e-shot target. The reason that this is a bad time is that many companies finish early on a Friday. When the client returns on Monday morning your e-shot will be amongst a lot of junk email that the client will probably delete without too much thought.

The best time to write an e-shot is after core sales time which is first thing in the morning, during lunch or after 17.00. The best time to send an e-shot is about 9.00, so it sits at the top of your client's inbox and is not sandwiched in between a bunch of other marketing emails. This way when they get into their office and open their emails it'll be right there at the top. You may want to play with different times to find that sweet spot. If you're sending e-shots to clients in other countries then work out the time so that when you send an e-shot it arrives in your client's email inbox at about 9.00 their time.

DID YOU GET MY E-SHOT?

Sending an e-shot at the beginning of the day is a good way to set up your telephone marketing for the day. You can call your clients and ask them what they thought of the e-shot you sent. It doesn't matter if they've read it or not. The objective is to use it as an excuse to call them and identify if they're currently recruiting. Don't forget to ask them insightful questions too.

BOUNCE BACKS AND OUT OF OFFICE REPLIES

If you receive email bounce backs, you'll need to look at why you're getting them. Have you spelt the email address wrong? Is it an old email address? Has the person got married and changed their name? Is the client information out of date? Call the reception of the company and ask them to confirm the email address with you. Even if a company has a policy of not providing email addresses the receptionist will still correct it for you, because they'll assume your client is expecting your email. Make the necessary corrections so that you know your e-shots are sending out correctly.

If you receive any out of office replies, make sure you read them and capture any important information, such as: direct lines, mobile numbers and names of other people you could sell to.

The Do's of E-shots

- Do make sure e-shots are sector specific
- Do direct e-shots at the right management level
- Do tailor e-shots into the appropriate format
- Do use language that is persuasive, professional and relevant
- Do check spelling and grammar is correct
- Do ensure they're compact and as short as possible
- Do have an option to opt-out
- Do send them to a client once a month

The Don'ts of E-shots

- Don't copy and paste a candidate's CV without tailoring it
- Don't spam your clients
- Don't send them on Friday afternoons
- Don't rush the production of them with bad spelling and grammar
- Don't be cheesy and write subject titles such as "The best candidate ever!"
- Don't send e-shots of candidates to the same company they're working at

PERSONAL BRAND

Your personal brand is how the world and society perceives you and it's no different from a corporate brand. When you look at corporate brands like McDonalds, you know wherever you are in the world the food will taste the same and you'll get the same level of customer service. If you take the time to consider more brands, you'll realise that some you'll perceive as trustworthy, some brands you'll think are fun, while others you'll perceive as reliable. Corporations market their brand in such a way to attract a certain target market.

If you want to be a rich recruitment consultant you'll need to take control and invest in your personal brand to the same extent as a large corporation does.

Firstly, as a recruitment consultant, you'll appreciate how important first impressions are. When you meet a candidate you're judging them as soon as you see them. How they carry their body language and how they dress. Do they smile? Are they confident? Would a client like them? On the other side when a client or candidate meets you for the first time they're also assessing you. Can this person recruit for me and represent my company in the best light? Can this person get me a job?

They're also subconsciously assessing your LinkedIn profile, your job adverts, your emails, your e-shots and your telephone calls just as you are with them.

The recruitment company you work for will have a corporate brand, but in the long term, clients and candidates work with individual recruitment consultants rather than recruitment agencies. Therefore, your personal brand can be considered as more important than the company's brand.

How you want to be perceived by your clients and candidates will be affected by the industry you work in, but also how you want to be perceived. In all cases, as a minimum, you'll want to be perceived as professional, trustworthy, reliable and confident.

DRESS TO IMPRESS

Your target market and your company policy will influence how you dress. To be seen as professional you'll need to invest in a couple of nicely fitted suits. Clients and candidates subconsciously know that if you can take care of yourself, you can take care of them. Imagine if you called the police and a police officer arrived in an ill fitted uniform with his shirt hanging out of his trousers. You probably wouldn't have much faith in their ability to solve your problem.

If you dress well, have a nice haircut and clean hands you'll feel good about yourself and you'll feel confident. Clients and candidates can sense this and will accept you more easily. You don't have to buy expensive suits, just ones that are well fitted and look smart. At the same time, don't wear any overly expensive jewellery otherwise clients will think they're paying you too much. While you want to give the impression of success and confidence you don't want to come across as arrogant. There is a big difference between confidence and arrogance, but many people confuse the two, or they act arrogant believing they're acting confident.

BODY LANGUAGE

We've touched on body language earlier in the book, but how you carry your body language is very important. The study of body language is a book in itself and I recommend you read into the subject, but for this book we'll just touch on the subject.

Every time you meet a client or candidate walk straight with your head up, make eye contact and smile, especially if you're walking into a room. Clients and candidates will instantly perceive you as confident.

When visiting a client, use the same body language that you would use in a job interview. Don't slouch or put your elbows on the table, and don't chew chewing gum. Also don't use too much dominant body language such as spreading yourself out. It's the client's territory not yours, so you should respect their domain. You should have open body language, so that your client and candidates can open up to you. Open body language means head up, legs uncrossed, and arms uncrossed. Don't touch your face or hide behind your hands. As the meeting goes on you can copy their body language to build trust. However, keep this relative. If the client puts their arms behind their head and leans back in the chair with their feet on the table, this doesn't mean you should do the same. By all means show that you're relaxed, but maintain your professionalism.

ACTIONS AND PROMISES
One of the most important tools for your personal brand is your actions. If you say you're going to call someone call them as promised. If you say you're going to email someone then ensure you do. Basi-

cally the rule of thumb is: do what you said you are going to do, and keep to your promises.

ONLINE BRANDING

Your LinkedIn profile should match your personal brand, so look at your profile picture and what you're wearing and doing. A picture of you on holiday drinking a cocktail may look pretty, but does this correlate with a confident professional recruitment consultant who can get the job done?

You should wear a suit in your profile picture and if possible try and get a professional picture. The content of your LinkedIn profile should sound sharp and confident with your contact details displayed so clients and candidates can reach you.

You'll also want to give the impression you're well connected. Currently LinkedIn only shows a profile as having equal or less than 500 connections, or having 500+ connections. You should aim to have 500+. This is not only for perception, but the more connections you have the more you'll come across clients and candidates to contact.

We've gone into detail about writing job adverts, but to recap on some key points your job adverts should be free from spelling mistakes and grammatical errors. They should sound appealing and always have your name and contact details on the bottom.

Blogs are a fantastic way to express your "professional" opinion and "expert knowledge" on relevant topics. Notice I said "professional" opinion. For example, writing a blog criticizing how the current government's policies are preventing job creation will only damage your personal brand. However, writing a blog how clients and candidates can solve problems caused by current government policies will cause you to be seen as an expert. If you write blogs, and I recommend that you do, they should go out at the same time every week or month, so people can see you as someone who's consistent.

The recruitment agency you work for will probably have a company website, but if you want your personal brand to become stronger than the brand of the company you work for then I recommend a personal website that shows your skills and services in a professional light. It should correlate and work in harmony with your company's website, but clients and candidates will be able to see you as an individual and understand your personal brand. Remember clients build relationships with individual recruitment consultants, not recruitment companies.

There are many websites that enable you to build a website cheaply with very little technical skill. Check out Word Press and Joomla. On your website, show your professional background, have links to your blogs, put up videos, show your contact details so people can contact you and send you CV's. Personalise it so your brand shows through. You may need to get the permission of your manager first before you do this.

Planning For Success

As I keep reminding you, you're extremely busy. You've got targets to meet, calls to make, e-shots to write, CV's to format, emails to send, candidates to interview, meetings with clients, references to chase, internal meetings to attend, all of which is on an endless cycle.

You'll at times feel stretched and stressed, but there are ways to manage this. This section of the book will help you manage your time more effectively. We've discussed several times how important being relaxed is. Being relaxed will enable you to negotiate better, make better sales calls, help you spot opportunities and it'll help you live a healthier life.

When you have everything organised and your day planned you'll feel relaxed and you'll feel in control. A sense of control will help you reduce those stress levels.

RECRUITMENT TIMETABLE

Mondays, especially Monday mornings are probably not the best time for sales. This isn't so much a limiting belief other than most people are on a come down from the weekend. However, while it's probably not best for sales calls, it's great for candidate calls. While people will be on a come down from the weekend and not wanting to listen to sales calls they'll be more than willing to discuss opportunities for a new job. Therefore, I recommend that Mondays should be dedicated to recruiting and keeping in touch with candidates. To contradict myself, this may not apply to your recruitment sector. For example, if you recruit for industrial or commercial personnel Monday may be a great day to do sales, especially after a big sporting event.

This can be a scary thought. You're probably thinking you've got sales targets to meet. The point isn't to meet sales targets but to fill placements. You'll learn more about the job market and current opportunities when you speak to candidates. Reread the section: Spotting Opportunities and Finding Leads. Candidates will tell you about jobs they've been put forward for by other agencies and they'll tell you how they're finding the market. I'm not suggesting you do no sales calls on a Monday, but the majority of your time should be focused on your candidates.

Telephone sales are best between 9.30 and 12.00 and then 14.00 to 17.00 these are known as your core hours. The reason for this is any calls between 9.00 and 9.30 may aggravate the client if they've just arrived at their desk. However, you should put some calls in before 9.00 and after 17.00 to sneak past gatekeepers and PAs, so you can catch hard-to-reach clients. Usually people take a lunch break between the hours of 12.00 and 14.00, so you're less likely to get clients on the phone. This can be frustrating. Instead use this time to speak to candidates, send emails, write CV's, create e-shots, interview candidates and any other administrative work. Again I'm not suggesting that you do no sales calls during this time, but your focus should be on more productive activities.

In the mornings before core hours I recommend sending e-shots, speaking to a couple of candidates and taking the time to plan your day, which we'll discuss in the next section.

After 17.00 use this time to interview candidates, make candidate calls, prepare CV's and write e-shots.

Try to work smarter, not necessarily longer. For example on a late Friday afternoon when clients generally finish early, don't use this time to do face-to-face interviews with candidates. Interviews take up a large amount of time. Instead use this time to call candidates and to set up the following week. This would involve creating all your e-shots and CV's to spec out. Also use this time to evaluate where you are on your targets and how close you are to earning commission. Then plan what you'd need to do to achieve your targets and hit commission in the following week.

DAILY PLAN

A daily plan is exactly what it says, it's a plan of what you're going to do and what you want to achieve for the day.

This doesn't need to be complicated, and it could be as simple as:

Target:

- 15 client calls
- 2 client meetings booked
- 2 candidate registration meetings
- 5 candidate calls
- Send an e-shot
- Get 1 new job on

How I'll achieve this:

- Send an e-shot in the morning
- Speak to 2 candidates before 9.30
- Speak to 10 clients in the morning
- Speak to 1 candidate at 12.30
- Interview candidate at 13.00
- Speak to 5 clients in the afternoon
- Recruit 2 new candidates after 17:00
- Book 2 client meetings
- Book 2 candidate registration meetings

You'll probably be given monthly targets. If you break these targets down into daily targets they'll be more manageable. Then if you stretch your daily targets by a small amount you'll massively exceed your targets over the month and increase your chances of winning new business. At the same time if for any reason you fall behind you'll be able to assess why. Don't just review your plan at the end of the day review it half way through the day to see if you've achieved what you planned in the morning. Seeing what you've achieved in the morning will help you create a positive mentality for the afternoon.

Summary

W e've come far together and I hope you've enjoyed the read. I would take great pleasure in knowing if you've found the book useful and if it's helped you to make a placement. I welcome any improvements, suggestions, war stories, or if you just want to get in touch, please feel free to contact me by going to the website:

www.therichrecruiter.com

You'll also find free resources there.

To get the best out of this book read it more than once and refer to it when you face challenges. There's so much to take in that it's easy to forget the basics.

Recruitment is a fun, fast paced industry, but it's also fiercely competitive. I urge you to never stop practicing your verbal and written sales skills. Keep practicing objection handling techniques with your colleagues and continue your learning.

Before you go, do you know anyone else who might benefit from reading this book?

Kind regards,

Andrew Leong

References &
Bibliography

Bettger, F. (2003). *How I Raised Myself from Failure to Success in Selling*. London: Simon & Schuster

Berkley, S. (2004). *Speak To Influence. How To Unlock the hidden Power Of Your Voice*. New Jersey: Campbell Hall Press

Blick, D. (2011). *The Ultimate Small Business Marketing Book*. Surrey: Filament Publishing Ltd

Cassell, J and Bird, T. (2012). *Brilliant Selling*. Edinburgh: Pearson Education Ltd

Collins, G. (2012). *Successful Selling*. Warwickshire: Easy Steps Ltd

Cooper, I. (2012). *Business Development How to win profitable customers and clients.* Edinburgh: Pearson Education Ltd

Etherington, B. (2006). *Cold Calling For Chickens.* London: Marchall Cavendish

Girard, J. (2006). *How To Sell Anything To Anybody.* London: Simon & Schuster

King, G. (2010). *The Secrets of Selling.* 2nd ed. Harlow: Pearson Education Ltd

Lowndes, L. (2003). *How To Talk To Anyone.* London: Element

Pease, A and Pease, B. (2005). *The Definitive Book of Body Language.* London: Orion Books Ltd

Rackham, N. (2012). *SPIN - Selling.* Surrey. Gower Publishing ltd

Townsend, H. (2011). *Business Networking.* Edinburgh: Pearson Education Ltd

Wiseman, R. (2004). *The Luck Factor.* London: Arrow Books

Zanker, B. (2012). *Think Big.* New York: William Morrow